Hands-On Research

Simplifying the Process

Second Edition

DISCARD

Lisa Shaw
Jennie Olaguibel-Lundahl

Miami Dade College

Kendall Hunt
publishing company

Cover image © Photodisc

Copyright © 2008, 2010 by Kendall Hunt Publishing Company

ISBN 978-0-7575-8666-8

gift   1792359   3/11

Contents

Our Vision for This Book

You are probably wondering why you have been asked to purchase yet another textbook for your English course because most likely you have already bought a handbook and a reader. Both the handbook and the reader are staples of every composition course, with the handbook taking on more significance in a second-level composition course with a research focus. While those books contain excellent research models and guides and provide an interesting variety of topics for research and discussion, we have noticed that semester after semester, our students have demanded additional practice and hands-on experience to more effectively prepare them for and walk them through the research process step-by-step—hence, the birth of this more experiential research companion.

As professors teaching the research paper, we have recognized that our students have expressed frustration and confusion with the same topics every semester: conducting searches; evaluating sources; taking notes properly; crediting sources properly; integrating borrowed material; avoiding plagiarism; and planning, organizing, drafting, and revising their own research papers. While the handbooks have provided examples and basic instructions, they did not provide enough actual practice to give students the confidence to independently prepare their own papers. This book is designed specifically to:

- Clarify in-class and traditional handbook material
- Provide opportunities for practice
- Provide supplemental assignments for practice
- Provide templates for your own research paper
- Offer step-by-step guidance through each phase of the research paper
- Answer the questions most frequently asked by students planning and writing a documented paper
- Provide a glossary addressing research-related vocabulary

How to Use This Book

This book is designed as a companion text to your class assignments. Our hope is that it will clarify the ideas, terminology, and individual steps of the research process you are undertaking in your composition class. The book is organized to correspond with the research process as it is taught in your class.

We begin with a definition of *research* to help you better understand what research is so you feel more comfortable with the task—from brainstorming ideas for possible topics through conducting searches (where to find information, how to determine the validity of sources), extracting information to take valuable notes, incorporating material into your paper, properly formatting citations, drafting, and revising. We have added a glossary at the back of the book to assist you in defining and remembering key research terms that your professor will be using throughout the course. When you have questions about a particular research skill, you will be able to find information and answers using the table of contents, arranged by topic. When topics overlap, you will be referred to a different section. For example, if you are looking for assistance with paraphrasing, you might find it in two locations: taking notes and plagiarism.

All of the worksheets we included can be detached and submitted according to your professor's requirements; and most of the templates for note taking, outlining, and drafting can be easily transferred to the research packet or final paper you submit.

Use this book as a blueprint for your success. Because research is a time-consuming, multistep activity, this book equips you with various opportunities to practice the same skill until you master it confidently. In some cases, you may want to photocopy the templates for additional practice.

Understanding the Research Process

Students at colleges throughout the United States confront the word *research* in their second-level English composition courses, approaching the dreaded "research paper" with anxiety and hesitation. Relax. Research is not as foreboding an experience as you anticipate, and to academic geeks like the authors of this book, it is actually fun. Yes, *fun.* How can that be?

It is all in one's perception. Research is actually an investigation, a thematic scavenger hunt of sorts, a verbal "connect-the-dots" activity. If a movie, television program, book, article, or even a conversation ever sparked in you a question that had no immediate answer, you were in the beginning stages of research. That is all research is: paying heed to your natural curiosity, formulating a question, determining where to find the answers, locating those answers, recording them, and presenting them in writing. For example, after watching a television documentary about slavery in America, you might want to know how society was able to "right" an indisputable historical "wrong." You might think further that civil rights legislation did not compensate for the horrors of two hundred years of slavery and begin questioning other methods of healing the wounds inflicted by such a process. You can explore the question of reparation for slavery, a hotly debated contemporary issue. Is it feasible? Is it necessary? Is it extreme or idealistic? Recognizing the different sides of the argument would be the beginning of research. Another current example would be the question of how a U.S. president is elected. Following the confusion and discontent over voting questions and alleged improprieties that arose during some past presidential elections, you might ask, "Is there a more effective way for us to vote for president?" or "Would an election based on popular vote be better for the country than the current electoral college system of voting?" These are questions that would lead into research, and research itself leads to discovery. That is the purpose of research. Begin questioning situations you encounter in your daily life. Did someone cut you off on the expressway this morning? Did you respond to the driver with a silent expletive or a visible gesture? How is it you were able to contain yourself even if agitated when others cannot? This can lead to your thinking about road rage. How common is it? Where is it most prevalent? What conditions contribute to it? Again, this is the beginning of a research project.

Basically, research is:

- A multistep project, not a single paper, to be completed over the course of six to eight weeks
- An investigation into an area that interests you
- A paper in which you present a thesis and support it with information from reputable sources and authorities on the subject

Pretest

1. What does MLA stand for?

   _____

   _____

   _____

2. How do you list the authors in a works cited page when you have two authors with the same last name?

   _____

   _____

   _____

3. What is an academic database?

   _____

   _____

   _____

4. Write the title of an article you have retrieved from a database.

   _____

   _____

   _____

5. Write the journal/magazine title of one of your researched articles.

   _____

   _____

   _____

6. What does *parenthetical* or *internal citation* mean?

   _____

   _____

   _____

7. What is the definition of *plagiarism?*

   _____

   _____

   _____

8. What is a *signal phrase?*

   _____

   _____

9. Directly quote two or three lines from one of your researched articles.

_____

_____

_____

10. Using a signal phrase, paraphrase the quotation from question 9.

_____

_____

_____

11. How are the entries arranged on a works cited page?

_____

_____

_____

12. What is the difference between a journal and a magazine?

_____

_____

_____

13. What is a periodical?

_____

_____

_____

14. What does "et al." mean?

_____

_____

_____

15. What type of documentation style will your research paper follow?

_____

_____

_____

16. What is the proper way to indent a works cited entry?

_____

_____

17. Give an example of a parenthetical citation.

_____

_____

_____

18. What is the MLA capitalization rule for article titles?

_____

_____

_____

19. What is never an accepted source in scholarly research?

_____

_____

_____

20. Why is Wikipedia not usually considered the most valid and reliable source of information on which to base research papers?

_____

_____

_____

Chapter  1

Beginning the Research Process

Brainstorming: Finding a Topic That Will Work

The most valuable advice we can give you regarding research is to investigate a subject that interests you. Because the research project will take approximately six to eight weeks, you are going to feel "married" to this topic, which will occupy your time not only in your English class but outside of class as well. If you are not completely invested in the subject you have chosen to research, you will not be excited about searching for material, finding information, and using it in your paper. Therefore, the initial step in identifying a suitable topic would be to examine your own interests. Your professor most likely has a preference for social, political, cultural, or literary topics, so make sure you clarify that before you begin.

To find a topic, look at your own preferences. Suppose that you plan to purchase a car within the next six months. Of course, you know your own tastes; but today, buying a car means more than just accessorizing by choosing a "hot" car in a flashy color. Consider the escalating costs of fuel, the amount of driving you do regularly, and the money you have available for car expenses. With the increasing frequency of the call to "go green," in terms of purchasing a car, that means considering hybrid vehicles.

Elaborating on the example of purchasing an automobile, consider the following questions.

- *What do I know about hybrid cars?*

  They supposedly get better gas mileage than standard fuel vehicles. They reduce emissions and the effects of pollution. They cost less to run than traditional vehicles, but they cost more to purchase. The federal government has been giving tax credits of $2,000.00 to people who purchase hybrids.

- *What do I not know about hybrid cars?*

  How long have they been on the road? What was the first commercial hybrid car? Is there still a waiting list to order one? What is the price range? How safe are they? How different are they to operate and run? Do hybrids really make an environmental difference? Do manufacturers make hybrid trucks?

1

- *What would I like to know about hybrid cars?*

  How reliable are they? How safe are they? What kind of maintenance do they require? How have they been tested and proven? How much of a difference in fuel economy can I expect with a hybrid car? Who manufactures them and what do they cost? Are they really cost-effective in the long run?

After examining this list of questions and its descriptions, you would formulate one question to help you refine your research topic.

- *Are hybrid vehicles easy on the pocketbook and on the environment?*

This is a good topic, but it is not phrased in a particularly academic way. It can be more formally posed.

- *What are the economic and environmental advantages of purchasing a hybrid vehicle?*

Reviewing, you may find this to be restrictive. Perhaps hybrid vehicles offer more advantages than just economic and environmental advantages. This is something you would find out as you gathered information during the research process. For now, you may be better off just asking the following question.

- *What are the advantages of owning a hybrid vehicle?*

On the following page is a brainstorming worksheet to help you identify your interests and list potential topics.

Brainstorming Worksheet

Name _____   **Date** _____

List four topics that interest you.

1. _____

2. _____

3. _____

4. _____

Now ask yourself which one of these four topics seems most exciting or interesting? Which seems familiar or overdone? (You may ask your professor to help you identify that one. Cross that one out.) When you look at the list, which of these topics emerges as one with the most potential to keep you interested? Which of these topics do you anticipate holds the most promise in terms of finding outside resources and information?

Write the topic here.

_____

Now write down what you already know about the topic.

_____

_____

_____

_____

Now write down what do you *not* know about the topic.

_____

_____

_____

_____

Now list a few things that you would *like* to know about it.

_____

_____

_____

_____

Formulate this as a concrete question.

_____

_____

Rephrase the question so that it has a more "academic" tone.

_____

_____

Narrowing Your Topic

Suppose that you want to do a paper on advertising. That is a huge subject; how will you be able to capture the subject in a brief paper? Chances are that your professor will assign a paper of five to ten pages, double-spaced, which is not a great deal of space to devote to such a huge topic. You will need to narrow the topic to a manageable subject. Following are a few possibilities that begin to reduce the enormity of the task. Next to each narrowed topic, identify possible subtopics that you could research and effectively address in a small paper.

Racism in advertising _____

Sex in advertising _____

Targeted marketing _____

Gender roles in advertising _____

Gender stereotypes in advertising _____

Physical perfection in advertising _____

Images of youth in advertising _____

A specific advertising technique _____

Celebrity endorsements_____

Racism in endorsements _____

Ageism in advertising _____

Advertising and female self-esteem _____

Research Schedule

Note: Fill in the due dates given by your professor.

Step	Complete By
Preliminary topic	
Refined topic	
First three to five sources	
Next three to five sources	
Bibliography cards	
Note cards	
Precis/abstract	
Topic outline	
Documented outline	
Rough draft	
Conference	
Final paper	

Identifying Sources

There are so many types of sources out there that it is virtually impossible to name them all here. But, you should be aware that besides the miles of books that your library may hold and the thousands of Web sites you have viewed through Internet searching, there is much, much more out there. The fact is, there is no shortage of information. However, the important question is, do you know where it exists? And more than that, do you know how to find it? Do you know the difference between a good source and one that really should not be used for a research paper? Though there is such a thing as "bad" information (meaning inaccurate information), what we want you to be most aware of is that there are certain types of information that are just more appropriate for certain assignments than for others. Recognizing what you need—and when—is a skill that you will refine as you develop your researching skills.

Books

First, you need to know what types of sources exist. Again, this list is only a beginning. While many students do not go to them first anymore, most of you are familiar with books. But note how many different "types" of books are printed.

- *Books with authors,* in which an individual or a few individuals (or even a company or organization) have contributed to one full-length work
- *Books with editors,* in which an individual or a few individuals have collected materials from various authors and compiled and edited them into a full-length work with a common theme, although each chapter is likely to be authored by a different individual or set of individuals
- *Anthologies,* books in which an individual or a few individuals have collected various works—usually literary pieces such as poems, short stories, plays, and so on that are written by various authors or even a single author—and have compiled all of the works into a single volume, usually arranged by theme or chronology
- *Translations,* books that were originally published by an author or authors in another language but were translated into English by an individual or set of individuals responsible for maintaining the accuracy of the information and its connotations as it changed language
- *Editions,* books in which original works were published but have since been revised, updated, and published again
- *Multivolume works,* a set of books from which the one book you use is only a part of several books related to that subject or theme which were all published together
- *Books in a series,* from which the one book you use is the first of many related to that subject or theme
- *Encyclopedias or dictionaries,* which are used primarily for background history or definition, are considered general reference material
- *Sacred books,* which are held in high regard by certain groups, usually used as guidance for religious belief systems

To be sure, this list does not include all the types of books there are; this is just a beginning list. But, it is a good beginning!

Periodicals

Periodicals are the next most common printed source. Unlike books, which usually take a fairly long time to move from the research to the writing and publishing, periodicals are shorter works that may take some time in researching but go through a faster process when it comes to publication; therefore, a periodical comes out more often. It comes out "periodically," meaning that it comes out at regular intervals—and how often it comes out depends on who is putting the material out and why. Some periodicals come out daily (like a newspaper) or weekly or monthly (like a magazine). Some periodicals come out bimonthly, semiannually, or seasonally (such as journal articles). So, what are the most common differences between them?

- A *newspaper* is a collection of articles reflecting recent events or certain areas of interest to a community, primarily for informational purposes. This is usually the most up-to-date, but it is not meant to reflect long-term research, as events and trends change daily.

- A *magazine* is a collection of articles, stories, pictures, or other features that are primarily for entertainment value and that usually focus on human interests. They can even include some interviews or opinion editorial columns.

- A *journal* is a collection of academic papers usually published by discipline or subject; the collection primarily focuses on research findings in that particular field. A longer process is used to verify the material, because it is usually reviewed by several professionals in the field before publication, which is why journals are not usually daily or weekly periodicals. Even the most frequently published journal usually only comes out monthly.

As you can see, even the most common print sources—the ones you deal with every day—can have a lot of elements to them that you would need to understand in order to know the type of material with which you are working. That does not even begin to address the electronic sources!

Electronic Sources

With *electronic sources,* you have so many different types of materials that, even as this book is being written, new ones are being invented! But at this point, we will just touch on the ones most of you would know and with which you are likely to work. The most common types of electronic sources are Web sites, online books, online periodicals, and online academic databases.

- Most students are familiar with *Web sites.* They are often the number one choice for researching by students! However, knowing what exactly a Web site is and the difference between them is not often something students can explain. It matters, though. If you are going to base your research on a Web site, then it is something you should be able to identify. Web sites are most often HTML pages that are created by "Web masters" in order to share information on the World Wide Web, or the Internet. The creators of the information are not usually the Web masters; those are usually separate individuals that specialize in HTML language in order to "publish" the information on the Web. The content is not usually regulated by the Web masters, though. It is usually created by an author or corporation or organization that wants to share information. The point is, you may have noticed how many types of Web sites there are but may not have realized how to distinguish between them. The following list separates them a bit.

  - A government Web site is usually created by a local, regional, or national governmental organization that is trying to share necessary public information such as laws, tax guidelines, school information, license requirements, and so on. Most of these Web sites have a URL (Web address) that ends with .gov.

  - A nonprofit Web site is usually created by an organization that is interested in generating information as a public service in order to assist in areas such as health, environment, and education. Most of these Web sites have a URL (Web address) that ends with .org.
    *Note: Although Wikipedia is a .org, it does not quite fit into this category. Because it is user-controlled and updated, it is not verified by a public organization, so it would not be as reliable as other .org Web sites.

- An educational Web site is usually created by an organization to share academic information, usually generated by colleges and universities, commonly meant to assist in several areas of education, such as working with academic skills or pursuing formal education. Most of these Web sites have a URL (Web address) that ends with .edu.

     *Note: Remember that college students may also construct .edu Web sites; therefore, it is still important to verify who has posted the information. A student paper may be good with interesting sources, but you would not want to base your research on another student's work. Doctoral dissertations may be an exception.

- A commercial Web site is usually created by an individual or business that wants to offer a service or product to the public and is usually in competition with a similar individual or business. The ultimate goal of these Web sites is usually some type of profit in some way, even if it is just in the advertising value of the product or service. Most of these Web sites have a URL (Web address) that ends with .com or .net.

- *Online books, or e-books,* are still not as common as print books, but they are becoming more and more widely available. With the more common distribution of e-book readers, this type of source is becoming more mainstream. Online books are books that are either written to be published solely online or they are books that have been published in print and now are available in an online version. The most popular online books are usually the books available for research and academic purposes as they are usually free and have been reviewed by an academic institution, but many bookstore Web sites are now offering e-book versions of popular titles for purchase.

- *Online periodicals* are also becoming more and more widely available. Online periodicals have newspaper, magazine, or journal articles that are written to be published solely online. These periodicals follow the same patterns as the print versions as far as content and publication process; they have simply bypassed the print publication process and were put directly online. They also usually have a wider audience because they are most often free. Note: Blogs, Web sites, wiki pages, and social networking Web sites may be updated periodically by an author or authors but these are not usually considered academic resources and are not subjected to any type of publication review process.

- *Online academic databases* are usually accessed through a public or college/university library Web site, although some are available through the general Internet as well. Databases are collections of books, articles, government documents, and so on that have been reproduced for online availability. It is important to understand that these are *not the same* as online periodicals. They are reproductions of materials that have already been published, but they have been put online by a service in order for the public/students/scholars to have easier access to them. Most of the academic databases are filled with journal articles that have been reviewed for their academic value.

- *Online web logs, or blogs* as they are more commonly known, are essays or analyses that appear as regular columns on the Internet. They can be very useful depending on the author of the blog. This means that questions of reliability and validity are that much more significant.

Are there other types of electronic sources besides these? There certainly are; however, as a beginning researcher, you are most likely to encounter the ones we have listed.

Other

There are also sources out there that are not considered print nor electronic and are sometimes classified as *other,* such as government publications, pamphlets, conference proceedings, and unpublished dissertations. It is a lot to distinguish.

For now, though, just try to notice the difference between the materials you are using. You need to recognize what kinds of sources you are using to find the most valid and reliable ones for building your paper.

Identifying Sources Activity

Name _____   **Date** _____

Identify each type of source that follows and explain how you were able to identify it.

1. Tumulty, Karen, and David Von Drehle. "Ready to Rumble." *Time*. 17 March 2008: 29–32.

2. Roll, John M., et al. "Cognitive Ability as a Factor in Engagement in Drug Abuse Treatment." *American Journal of Drug and Alcohol Abuse,* 8/1/05.

3. "Mortgage Crisis Crosses the Atlantic Subprime Loans and Foreclosures Affecting Everyone." 13 March 2008. http://www.cbsnews.com/stories/2008/03/13/uttm/main3937617.shtml

4. Sparrow, Joshua. "What's All the Fuss?" *Parent & Child*. December 2007: 36.

5. O'Brien, Tim. "The Things They Carried." *The Vietnam Reader*. Ed. Stewart O'Nan. New York: Anchor Books/Doubleday, 1998: 593.

6. "Obama Takes the South." *Sun-Sentinel*. 5 March 2008: A1.

7. "Students Rally on Capitol Hill for More Support of Higher Education." *The Chronicle of Higher Education*. 19 March 2008. http://chronicle.com/daily/2008/03/2169n.htm

Identifying Sources: Quiz

Name _____   **Date** _____

1. What is a periodical?

    _____

2. Give two examples of types of periodicals.

    _____

    _____

3. A journal is usually specific to

    _____

4. How can you tell if an article was published in a newspaper?

    _____

    _____

5. EBSCO and Gale are examples of

    _____

6. Where would you find a microfilm and what type of information would you find on it?

    _____

7. Explain how a database functions.

    _____

    _____

8. What piece of information always identifies a source as a book?

_____

9. What type of source is *Newsweek*?

_____

10. http://www.findarticles.com is an example of a/an

_____

Chapter **2**

Searching for Sources

Source Validity

What does it mean to be *valid?* When you first think of the word, you may think of the term *real* or *true*. For many students, though, *source validity* takes a backseat to convenience. Often beginning researchers do not care if something is real or true—just as long as it says what the student wants it to say. While that may seem like a good idea at the time, if you really want to have quality work, you are going to have to base it on something more than convenience. Is the work really reflecting good research on what it is supposed to be analyzing? When you are going through your sources—whether they be books, periodicals, or electronic— ask yourself a few questions about each one.

- What do I know about the person who wrote this? What are his or her qualifications?
- What method did the person use to get his or her results or reach his or her conclusions?
- What kinds of sources did the person cite in his or her work? Do the examples come from a study or from personal experience?
- Whom does the person represent? An academic institution? An organization? A corporation? A governmental division?
- How well does the author address alternative views? Are any included in this work?
- What kind of language does the author use? Is it respectful and fair?

The following worksheet can be used to analyze any source you find during your research process. Tear out the sheet and make as many copies as you need in order to answer these questions for each source you consider using.

Source Worksheet—Validity

Name _____ **Date** _____

Source _____

1. What do I know about the person who wrote this? What are his or her qualifications?

   _____

   _____

2. What method did the person use to get his or her results or reach his or her conclusions?

   _____

   _____

3. What kinds of sources did the person cite in his or her work? Do the examples come from a study or from personal experience?

   _____

   _____

4. Whom does the person represent? An academic institution? An organization? A corporation? A governmental division?

   _____

   _____

5. How well does the author address alternative views? Are any included in this work?

   _____

   _____

6. What kind of language does the author use? Is it respectful and fair?

   _____

   _____

Source Reliability

What does it mean to be *reliable?* When you are able to *rely* on someone, it means you can count on them to always be there. *Source reliability* is just as important. In other words, when you look at a source, you should see your author being consistent in his or her ideas. The author should be referring to the same conclusions as you read through the work; and across your sources, you should be seeing some things in common. That does not mean that all authors have to reach the same conclusion. It does mean, however, that there should be threads of commonality. You should be able to count on your sources to be consistent and not reach a different conclusion each time the idea is being studied—that is, you should not have ten different conclusions for ten different authors. If you have a series of sources side by side, and one of them is reaching some way out conclusions that none of the others have even mentioned, you may not have the most reliable material in that one source. Just as with validity, be sure that what you are using to build your work is reliable, so that you too can be considered reliable as a beginning researcher. Again, ask yourself a few questions.

- How well does the author present his or her information? Is it organized? Clear? Logical?
- How well does the author build his or her ideas? Are there multiple details and examples to continuously affirm those ideas?
- How consistent are this author's findings in comparison to other sources you have found on this subject?
- How recent is the author's material? Are the sources cited up-to-date? Is it a landmark study?
- How well known is the source author or journal or book when it comes to publications on this subject?
- How well is this work written? Is it error-free in grammar, mechanics, and usage?

As with validity, the following worksheet can be used to analyze any source you find during your research process. Tear out the sheet and make as many copies as you need in order to answer these questions for each source you consider using.

Source Worksheet—Reliability

Name _____ **Date** _____

Source _____

   1. How well does the author present his or her information? Is it organized? Clear? Logical?

      _____

      _____

   2. How well does the author build his or her ideas? Are there multiple details and examples to continuously affirm those ideas?

      _____

      _____

   3. How consistent are this author's findings in comparison to other sources you have found on this subject?

      _____

      _____

   4. How recent is the author's material? Are the sources cited up to date? Is it a landmark study?

      _____

      _____

   5. How well known is the source author, journal or book when it comes to publications on this subject?

      _____

      _____

   6. How well is this work written? Is it error-free in grammar, mechanics and usage?

      _____

      _____

Abstracts

As you get ready to begin your search, now that you know the variety of sources that are out there for you to find, and you know how to evaluate them to some degree, you can shorten some of your search time if you learn to work with something called *abstracts*. Most students know abstracts as *summaries,* but they are meant to be a little more than that. It should be clarified here, though, that an abstract is *not* a source. While an abstract can contain a lot of pertinent information, it is meant to reflect a piece of work, not take its place.

In short, an abstract is usually about 150 words (or less in some cases), and it is meant to capture what the reader needs to know to understand the work, such as why the work is important, what steps were followed to create it, what the highlights are of each section, and what was concluded in the work. Notice that many of the validity and reliability questions can be answered just by reading the abstract.

Most abstracts are informative abstracts, and they are usually done for research articles that are published in academic journals; but they are also sometimes written for books and other print materials. Some academic databases are strictly abstracts, so you can decide what to look for next, so to speak, once you have reviewed multiple abstracts. They can save a lot of time if you look at them carefully; you need to know if any articles are worth pursuing.

Understanding Main Ideas

Understanding the main idea in any book, article, or electronic resource is very important. This is not the same thing as understanding the "details" of the work. Sometimes when students are asked what the main idea of a work is, they start to state different findings that the author has reached and different examples that the author has discussed. That is not what you want to start with when you first find a source that you have read and want to use. Initially, you need to ask yourself one question.

- What is the essential idea or concept around which this author framed the whole work?

Yes, there will be sections that will have their own "main ideas"; but look at the work overall, and imagine that you have to sum up the author's entire work in *one* sentence. Consider what that summary would be.

- What is this author's message? In other words, what does he or she want the reader to be sure to walk away knowing?

Once you have that, you can then go into each section of the work and find the core elements/topics/issues with which the author has built that main idea. Then, when you gather several sources, you can compare and contrast and find the commonalities on which you can build your paper. First, though, you have to analyze each individual source for what it has to offer. Then you will see the commonalities emerge.

Use the following worksheet for this analysis. Complete a worksheet for each source you are using. Make as many copies as you need for as many sources as you plan to have. Then begin to compare the worksheets to see what they have in common with each other. A sample worksheet follows as an example.

Source Analysis Worksheet

Name _____   **Date** _____

Source:
(Include all of the pertinent bibliographic information.)

_____

_____

_____

_____

Author's main idea:
(What conclusion has the author reached about this topic in this source?)

_____

_____

_____

_____

First subject author discusses:

   What is the author's main idea about this subject?

_____

_____

_____

_____

Second subject author discusses:

   What is the author's main idea about this subject?

_____

_____

_____

_____

Third subject author discusses:

　　What is the author's main idea about this subject?

_____

_____

_____

_____

How do all of these points support the author's main idea?

_____

_____

_____

_____

Sample Source Analysis Worksheet

Name _____   **Date** _____

Source:
"Finding Ways to Beat the Blues Drug-Free" by John Smith _____

_____

_____

_____

Author's main idea:
There are effective ways to beat depression without having to take prescription drugs. _____

_____

_____

_____

First subject discusses:
Side effects _____

_____ *What is the author's main idea about this subject?* There are way too many side effects with prescrip-

_____ tion medications that can hurt an individual mentally, physically, and emotionally. _____

_____

Second subject author discusses:
Money _____

_____ *What is the author's main idea about this subject?* Prescription medications are very costly, many people

_____ don't have the insurance to cover them, and they wind up in debt or with low-quality medication anyway.

_____

Third subject author discusses:

Family

    What is the author's main idea about this subject? Family members can be a very strong support system and can sometimes be just as effective as (in place of) prescription medications.

How do all of these points support the author's main idea?

All of the topics show that there are a lot of drawbacks to using medication, and there are alternatives that can be just as good.

Once you understand the variety of sources that are out there, then you are ready to try out a variety of methods to find good sources for your research paper. There are so many ways to find source material, and only some will be covered here, but what you have here is definitely sufficient to create a well-developed research paper.

Electronic Sources

Academic Databases

There is absolutely nothing wrong with using books or other print material as sources. In many cases, that is the best route to take when you are looking for a "collection" of research on a given topic in one book, or if you are looking for an in-depth longitudinal study published in an extended full-length work by an expert in the field. This may also be a useful approach if you are looking for a primary source like a government document or an original version of a speech and not just an excerpt, or if you want the most current publications possible of journal articles and newspapers. These other types of sources are approached in some detail later.

For now, though, you need to be introduced to academic databases. The use of academic databases is by far the most common academic method used by university students across the country. Notice that we said *academic* method. Many students are very attached to their "Google" and "Wikipedia" ways; and really, they are just fine to use if you know the difference between good academic research and unverified material, but you have to be exposed to the real thing first. This may feel uncomfortable initially only because when it comes to Google or Wikipedia, we know that we can type in *anything* and get some kind of result. No matter what subject you create in your mind, someone out there has created a Web site for it; but, once you adapt and learn the databases, they are much more precise and verifiable and can be a much faster tool if you learn how to go to the right database and use the right keywords and search methods. Every library these days subscribes to a set of databases whether general or academic. We'll model getting into academic databases through Miami Dade College's databases here, but chances are your library has similar steps. Just start with your library's homepage and go from there.

To get to the Miami Dade College (MDC) databases, just follow these easy steps.

- Go to *http://www.mdc.edu/north/library.*
- In the center of the page are several icons reflecting different things such as Catalog, Databases, Recommended Websites, Science Resources, and so on. Click on Databases.
- Once you click on Databases, click on Log in. Most colleges and universities will limit their databases to their students. Public libraries allow general public use with a library card number.

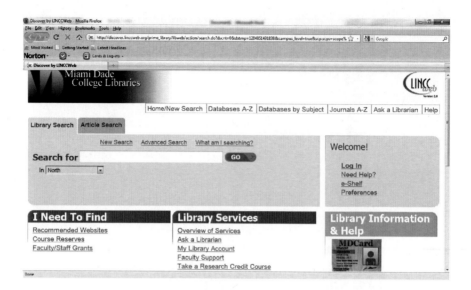

Most schools go by your full student ID number, but if you are not sure, there is usually a help link to clarify what your ID and pin should be.

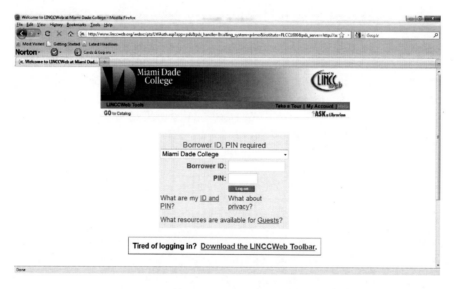

- Type in your borrower ID number (for MDC students, the ID is the nine-digit MDC student number on your schedule).
- Type in your PIN (for MDC students, it is the last four digits of that student number).

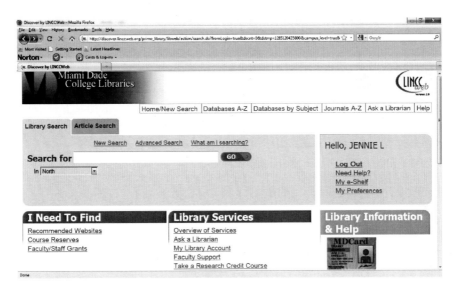

- Click on Databases A–Z at the top; you will then see a list of all the databases.

- Take a look at all of the possibilities. Some are subject-specific and others are what they call *multidisciplinary,* which means they include information on multiple subjects. Note: You can also click on databases by subject and see the databases for that subject.

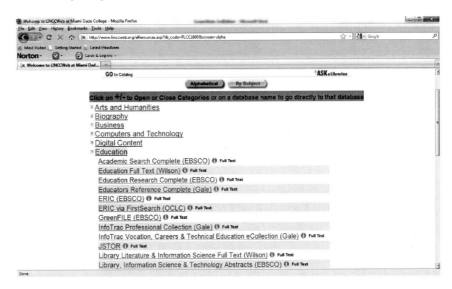

- Click on a database that fits with your topic or choose a multidisciplinary database which includes material on almost any subject.
- Click on Connect to Database.

Start your search with some basic tips in mind. Once you log in to the academic databases and you select and connect to a database, you will find blank fields that allow you to enter search terms. There is specific advice for navigating the different types of databases later in this chapter because they do vary in appearance and navigation technique, but the basics of searching still remain the same. Some general guidelines follow that you can use for any of them.

- Use only one or two words per search line. Do not put full sentences or long phrases. That will likely produce too narrow or no results.
- Keep a list of words you are using and in what combination. As you start searching, you will feel like you have used *everything*. This will help you keep track of what you have really used and help you add as you go along.
- As you search, try synonyms for your initial words and phrases. For example, if you mean *teenagers,* also use *adolescents, kids, children, youth,* and *teens.*
- Start with general terms. If you do not get a lot of results or very relevant results right away, it is best to broaden the words you are using. For example, if you are looking for *prayer in public institutions,* just search for *prayer* at first. Review the results. Then you can read a few abstracts and see what other words you can use to combine with the original term. You can also follow the subject links that those general results have produced. For example, after you see the results for *prayer,* you can try *prayer* and *schools* (which are a type of public institution) or follow a subject link that says *prayer in the U.S.* The more words you use, the more "narrow" the results, so you do not necessarily want to start with too many words.
- Be *patient.* For many of you, this is the first time you are researching and it may also be the first time you use academic databases. Take your time. Relax. It will not be instant. Do not search for less than twenty minutes or more than forty-five. If you search for more than forty-five minutes, then stop. Contact your instructor. Ask for suggested keywords. It does *not* mean there are no results out there just because *you* are not finding them. It just means you need someone more experienced to help you search with fresh words. Ask for help. Soon you will be the one giving advice.
- Once you find a great article, write down all the important bibliographic information of the source, but especially note the keywords you used to find the article and what database you found it in. By doing this, if something should happen while e-mailing it or printing it, you can find it again easily.

The first set of databases that you should use is the set that most students find is the easiest to work; that would be the Wilson databases. Wilson databases are very user-friendly in that they use easy-to-read icons and every Wilson database looks the same, which will not always be the case with the other types of databases. Please understand that Wilson is the service of this collection of databases; it is not just one database. And this collection houses hundreds of thousands of articles. There is plenty of material here.

Tips for Working with Wilson Databases

- Once you get to the list of databases, click on OmniFile Fulltext Mega to start. Then, click on Connect to Database. (*Note:* OmniFile has many subjects, so clicking on that one to start is always a good beginning; the others are additions that should be relevant to whatever topic you are doing.)
- Click on Open Database Selection Area at the top and check off any additional databases you think might also fit your subject. For most contemporary social issues, we often recommend selecting all education, business, legal, social science, and general science databases, in addition to the multidisciplinary database.
- Click and checkmark next to Limit to Peer Reviewed. (This will keep the results narrowed down to academic and scholarly sources.)

- Click and checkmark next to Limit to Full Text Articles. (This will allow you to print or e-mail the full article for yourself.)
- Click on Dates and limit dates to the last ten years. (For example, from year 2000 to year 2010—this will ensure that you have current information.)
- Keep it on Advanced Search. (This will allow you to combine keywords.)
- Keep it on All-Smart Search. (This will search abstracts, summary, and text for the words you are looking for.)
- Keep it sorted by Relevance.

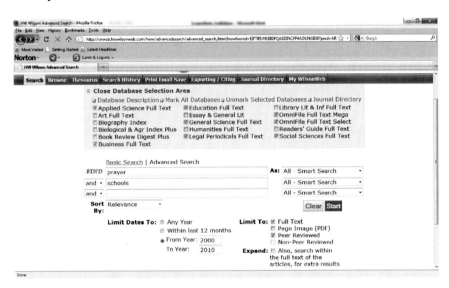

- Type in one to two words related to your topic to begin your search.
- Click on Start.
- Review results that are 70 percent relevant or higher. (If it falls below 70 percent, it is likely that it is not too related to what you are really looking for.)
- Note the symbols listed with each result. The graduation cap signals scholarly/peer reviewed results, and the small paper or red symbol indicates full text either in HTML version or via Adobe Reader (PDF). (If you do not see these next to your results, you may have forgotten to limit to full text and peer reviewed. Be sure you do this before you search. But, if you are already in the results, notice the tabs at the top. You can click on the "Peer Reviewed" tab; then it will light up in yellow, and you can look through the results with the full text icons.)

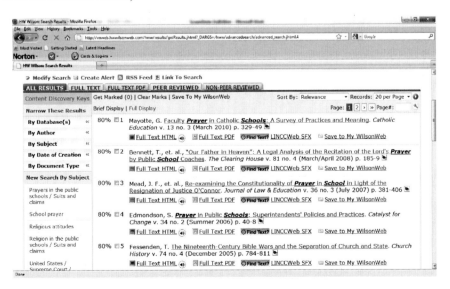

- *Note:* Since you clicked on Limit to Full text, all of your articles should be readily available. However, if you choose to search without limiting to full text and you like one that does not have a full text icon, click on Find Text.

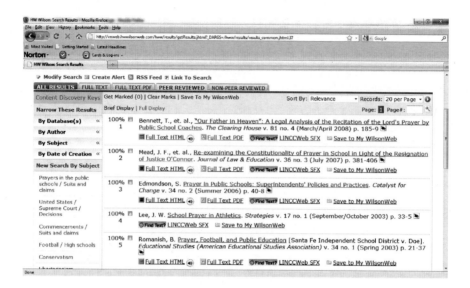

It will then usually take you to an SFX service which may take you to another set of databases to which your library subscribes that may have a copy of the article. Simply click the 'Go' button next to the new listings.

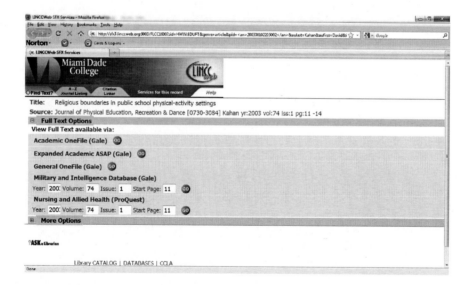

If the full text copy is available online it should take you right to it.

- For each result that you want to look into further, you can just click on the title of the article and review the abstract. When you review the abstract, which is the summary of the article, you can see if the material is relevant.

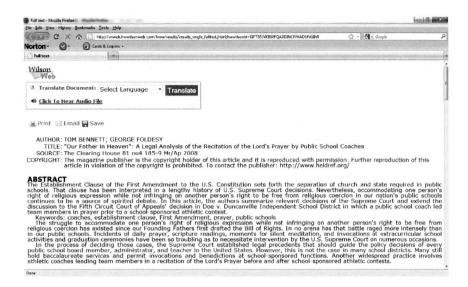

- Once you click on the full text link, it will usually show you the full text along with the abstract again as well as the option to hear an audio recording of the article, sometimes with a translation of the article in a choice of languages. This is not available for all articles, however.

- If you like an article, you can save and print it right away; to do this, simply click on the Save option at the top and save it to a flash drive or your desktop (to be e-mailed to yourself later), and/or you can click on the Print option at the top and print it out. Or you can e-mail it to yourself right away.

- If you know that the article is just one of many you may want to review before you decide, mark the article. Mark the article by going back to the list of results and checking the box next to the number of the result.

- You can also access additional results by looking at the "Suggested Subjects" listed on the side column. If you have marked all of the articles that you liked from your own keyword search, then click on one of these subjects. It will take you to a new list of results. *Please note:* When you get that new list, remember that you need to narrow it down to full text and peer reviewed as well. To do this, simply click on the "Full Text" tab (the tab will then turn yellow and all articles not full text will be taken out) and then click on the "Peer Reviewed" tab (this tab will also turn yellow and then any articles not peer reviewed will be eliminated). Or, as discussed earlier, leave the full text unclicked and use the SFX service to find the full text online.

Note: If you feel you have run out of ideas, click on Thesaurus at the top and type in your original keywords. Wilson will produce related records that you can click on and select as well.

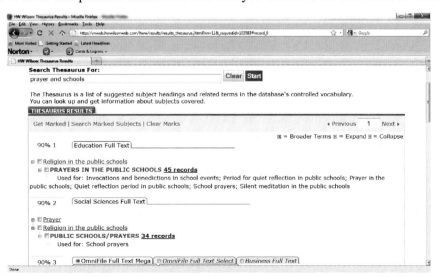

- Once you have reviewed and checkmarked all the articles you like, go to the top of the page and click on 'Get Marked.'
- Then, when you have the list of all the articles you have marked, go to the top of the page and click on the Print or E-mail or Save link. (E-mail is usually best, but consider also saving on a flash drive or printing as a backup.)
- Click on the E-mail link.

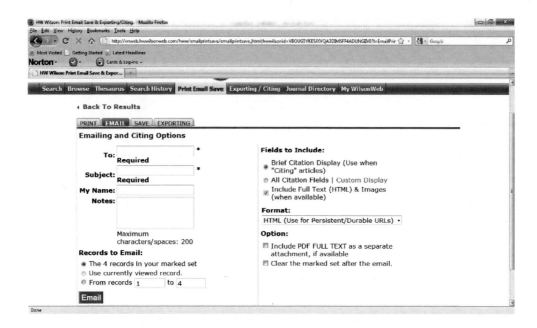

- Type in your personal e-mail address and subject of the e-mail.
- Type in your name, and in the notes, record what keywords you used and what Wilson databases you checked off.
- For Records, be sure it is marked next to Records in your Marked Set.
- For Fields, be sure you have selected All Citation Fields and be sure to have checkmarked Include Full Text.
- For Format, you can leave it on HTML or for a smaller file, click on Rich Text. (Note: You can also choose pdf full text as a separate file if you like.)
- Click Yes for "Clear the marked set after e-mail."
- Click on E-mail.
- Write down the confirmation number when the confirmation notice comes onto the screen.
- After clicking OK, go to the top of the screen and click on Search.
- You will return to your original search screen where you can now use new words to search.

  Note: You can also set up alerts at the end of your search such that any new articles published with those keywords will trigger an e-mail sent to you notifying you of its publication.

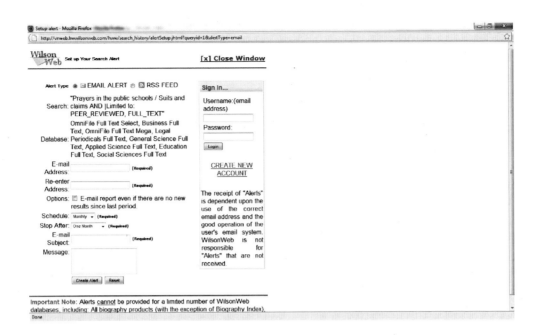

As you get used to the Wilson databases, you will find yourself more and more comfortable with searching and some of the norms of academic databases, so moving on to the next type of database is just a matter of transferring that knowledge you have of the old type to the new type, even if it looks a little different.

For additional help maneuvering the databases, go to iTunesU and download our podcasts with step by step instructions for navigating each database. Simply go to: http://deimos3.apple.com/WebObjects/Core.woa/Browse/mdc-public.3523749442.03523749444.

Another set you may use regularly beyond Wilson databases is the Gale databases.

Tips for Working with Gale Databases

- Start by clicking on Academic OneFile. It is a multidisciplinary database and therefore includes multiple subjects.
- After connecting to the database, it should already be on Advanced Search.
- Make sure it is limited to documents with full text. (This will allow you to print or e-mail the full article for yourself. However, as with Wilson databases, if you leave the full text option unchecked, you can use the SFX service to try to track down the article.)
- Limit to Peer Reviewed Publications. (This will keep the results narrowed down to academic and scholarly sources. *Note:* Because each Gale database may vary in appearance, you are looking for words like *peer reviewed, scholarly reviewed, research articles,* or *refereed publications.*)
- Limit to dates between 2000 and 2010. (This will ensure that you have current information.)
- Do not limit by title or subject or lexile reading level. You can, however, limit to article or other type of document depending on your search.
- Type in keywords to search.

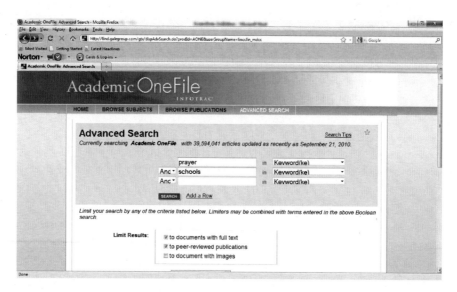

- When you get results, sort the results by Relevance. Because it automatically sorts by Publication date, click on it to change it to Relevance. This will ensure that it lists the results that are most related to your topic first.

- When you get results, note that next to the source information/page numbers, it will usually tell you how long the article is by total pages in parentheses or total words within the article. *Also note:* You most often want *article* results, not *book reviews, brief articles, letters,* or so forth, depending on the type of paper you are completing. Just be sure you are aware of the type of source with which you are working.

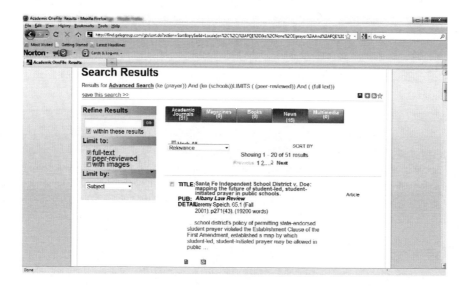

- Click on the HTML icon or the PDF icon to see the full article you think you might like. Review the abstract if it has one or the first couple of paragraphs to see if the material is relevant. If so, mark the article. (Also notice that like Wilson, within each article there is the option of printing, e-mailing, downloading and listening to the article. Sometimes there is also a translation of the article as well.)

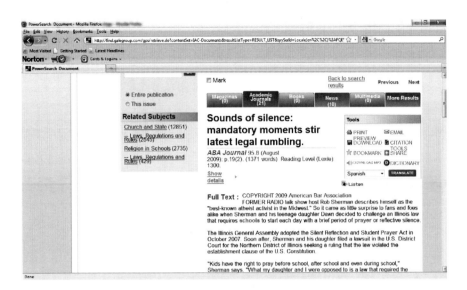

- Mark that specific article by checking the box at the top, above the article titles (or on the list of results) next to the result. You can always click on the word Results to go back to your full list of articles.

- Notice that when you go into a result in the Gale databases, you can also see Related Subjects in the left-hand column. As with Wilson databases, you can click on one of these subjects and get new results, but then remember to limit to Peer Reviewed and Full Text. To do this, simply be sure to click on the "Academic Journals" tab of the new results, and checkmark Peer Reviewed and Full Text; the database will then eliminate any sources that are not those things. (Or, if the full text option is unchecked, you can use the SFX service to try to track down the article. Click on Find Text.)

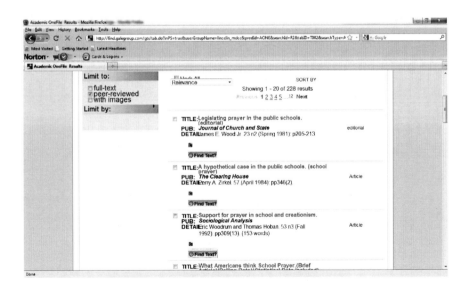

- Once you have reviewed and checkmarked all the boxes you like, go to the top of the screen and click on Marked Items (which is under the "Home" button).

- At the top, you will see the option to Print or E-mail (or on the left-hand side you will see the option to check and click on Download, which means to save the full text articles to a flashdrive and/or computer and/or floppy disk). *Note:* Whichever you use, be sure that Full Text is clicked on and if you have to choose a version, choose HTML or PDF if you expect to have the full article and/or its link e-mailed to you.

- If e-mailing, type in your personal e-mail address and subject of the e-mail along with any other requested information. (In the message, you may want to list the keywords you used to find these sources.)

- Be sure "Send All" is checked. Click on Send.

- The e-mail will arrive in your e-mail box from Gale Academic OneFile. (This may vary, depending on which Gale database you are in.)

- After you get the confirmation that your e-mail was sent, close the confirmation window. Then, at the top, click on Advanced Search.

- You will return to your original search screen where you can now use new words to search.

- If you are done with Academic OneFile, you can also click on Change Databases in the upper left-hand corner to conduct a power search of all Gale databases.

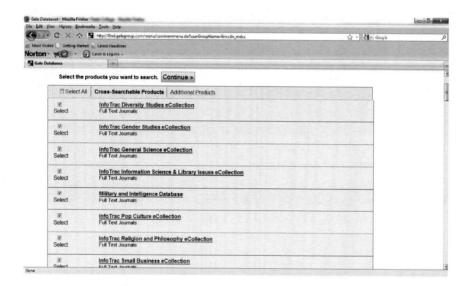

- When you do this, you will see a list of databases, many of which are already checked off. However, go through and uncheck any databases that would not be of use to you. For example, the database "Informe," which is a collection of Hispanic magazines, may not suit your topic, so you would uncheck that. Also note that some are for middle and high school students. Be sure to uncheck those.

- Then, type in your keywords. Use the word *and* to connect your keywords, such as *prayer and schools*.

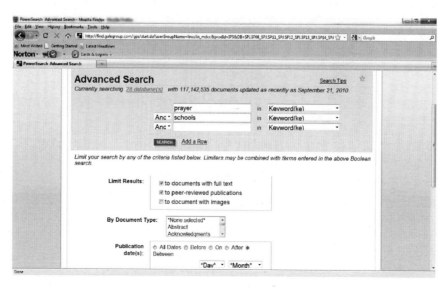

- When you get results, be sure to click on the academic journals tab; then click on Full Text so you can eliminate any that do not have the article immediately visible. Then, be sure to click on Peer Reviewed to eliminate any nonacademic results. (However, if peer reviewed is not required of you, notice how you also have video and blog results that can be used as sources in the multimedia tab.)

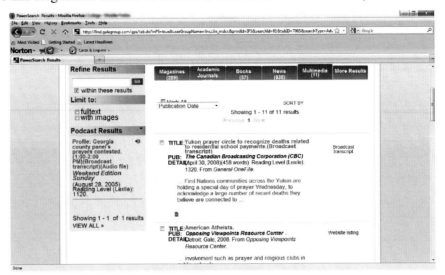

- Remember to sort by relevance.
- As before, mark articles to print, e-mail, or save.
- Then click on Advanced Search to start a new search.
- Alternately, there are additional Gale databases you may go into one by one. Click on Change Databases to go back to the list. As long as it is related to your topic, it is okay, as long as you remember to take familiar steps. Click on Advanced Search, look for Full Text and Peer Reviewed boxes to check off and limit the dates. Then, when you get results, you look for a way to mark the article, e-mail the article, and/or save the article. They may look differently but they work the same way.
- Keep practicing, and soon all of this will become an easy process!

Literary Searches

You can also conduct purely literary searches by going back into the Gale list of databases (remember to click on 'Change Databases') and choosing one of the Gale Literature databases. These searches would work a little differently from the non-fiction social issues search in that you can narrow the search by the author or work that you are choosing to research.

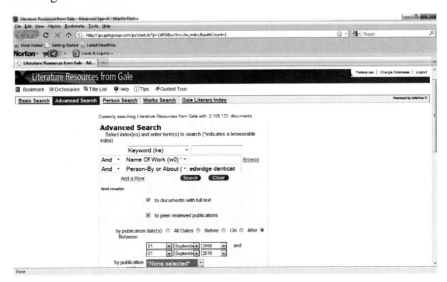

Also notice that when you get results, you can limit your search further by looking specifically into literary criticism, biographical information, overviews of the work, reviews of the work, primary sources regarding the work or even multimedia results regarding the work or the author. Simply click on the appropriate tab listed at the top of the search results. In addition, on the left-hand side you will have a list of works by the author you are researching so that you can narrow your search to a particular literary piece the author has created.

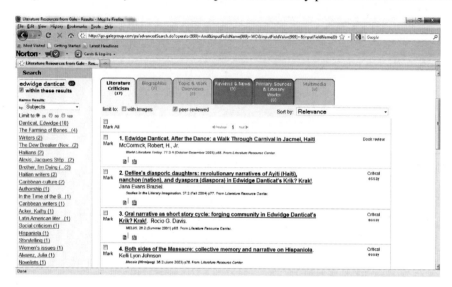

For additional help maneuvering the databases, go to iTunesU and download our podcasts with step by step instructions for navigating each database. Simply go to: http://deimos3.apple.com/WebObjects/Core.woa/Browse/mdc-public.3523749442.03523749444.

Another set of databases that you may use regularly is the EBSCO databases. Just like before, build on the knowledge you have acquired in the previous practices. When you look at the beginning EBSCO screen, remember what you have learned.

Tips for Working with EBSCO Databases

- After connecting to one of the multidisciplinary EBSCO databases, such as Academic Search Complete, click on the "Advanced Search" tab at the top. Leave the Default Fields.

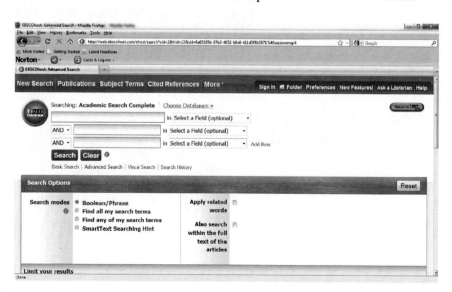

- Click on Choose Databases at the top. Select databases that you wish to search in by checking the box next to the name of the database. If you read the brief description for each database, you will know what it covers and if it is appropriate for your topic. Notice that some of these databases are designed for middle and high school students. Be sure to verify that the ones you are choosing are at the college level.

- Also notice that you can set limitations unique to each database. Just remember that the more you limit, the narrower your results will be.
- Limit to Full Text. (This will allow you to print or e-mail the full article for yourself. Remember that some may not have this option; choose it for the ones for which it will apply.) Those that do not have full text results will have the SFX service option available for you to be able to try to find it.
- Limit to Scholarly (Peer Reviewed or Refereed) Journals. (This will keep the results narrowed down to academic and scholarly sources. Again, most have this option, but if not, try to limit to research articles or articles with "references available" or "research article" for the most academic results.)
- Limit Published Date to the last ten years, such as Jan 2000 to Jan 2010. (This will ensure that you have current information.)
- Do not limit by publication name.
- Change Publication Type from All to Periodical if the database has that option for the most current material.
- Change Document Type from All to Article if the database has that option for the most immediate ideas on a topic.
- Do not choose Number of Pages or Cover Story. Do not limit to articles with images.
- Be sure to exclude book reviews or article abstracts; remember those can lead to sources but are not complete sources by themselves.
- Type in keywords to search.

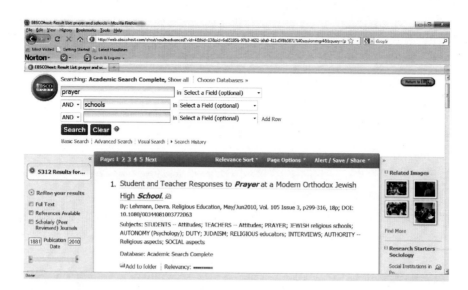

- When you get results, keep it sorted by Relevance. It should automatically be so; if not, click on it to change to Relevance, so that you can see which results are most related to the search words you used.
- Like in Wilson or Gale databases you can also search by related subjects on the left-hand side of the results or article.

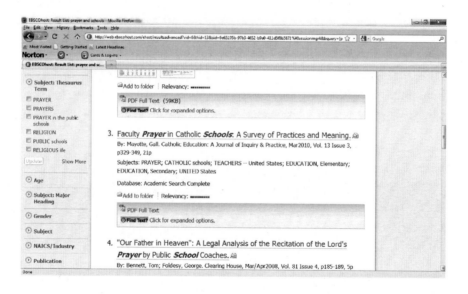

- Click on HTML or PDF or Linked Full Text to see the full article you think you might like. Or, if you click on the title, you can review the abstract if it has one to see if the material is relevant. You can also scan the initial paragraphs to see if your result is relevant. Your keywords will be in boldface.

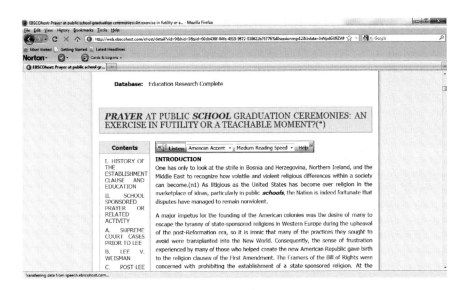

Note: For pdf files, you may also choose another article from the same journal issue.

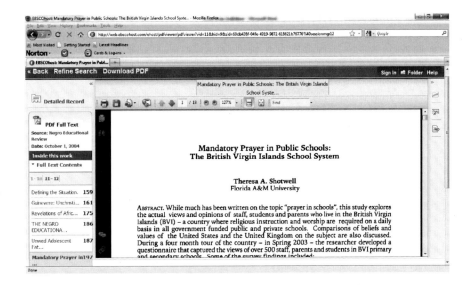

- If you like the source, click on Add to Folder at the right-hand side of the article or from the results list right under the source in order to put the article in the Folder.
- Always click on Result List to go back to the full list of results.

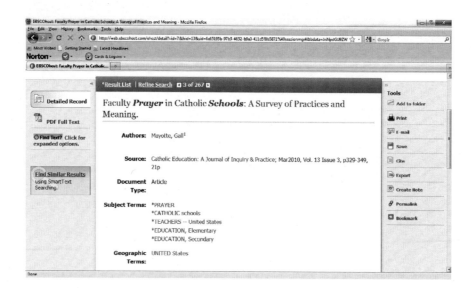

- Notice that like Wilson and Gale databases, you may print or e-mail or listen (for html files) to each article as you choose.

- As with Wilson and Gale databases, you have the option of following one of the subjects under the abstract to get new results. You may limit by Full Text and Peer Reviewed in the left-hand column if you choose.

- Once you have reviewed and "added" all the articles you like, go to the top of the page and click on Folder.

- Click select at the top of the list to choose all the articles in the folder.

- To the right of the list of added articles, you will see the option to Print or E-mail or Save. Whichever you choose, be sure to click on Detailed Citation and Abstract, HTML Full Text (or HTML Link to Full Text), and/or PDF as Separate Attachment (if available) in order to get all of the sources, not just the abstracts.

- If you are e-mailing, type in your personal e-mail address and subject of the e-mail. (You may want to type the keywords you used in the comments section so you can keep track of how you found them.)

- Select the option to remove items from the folder after you have e-mailed or saved them.

- Click on Send (or File or Save/Download).

- A confirmation that it has been sent will be shown. Click on Continue.

- There will be zero items in your folder.

- At the top, click on 'back' to go back to the search screen. You can now search again with new words.

Remember, the more you use these, the more familiar every step becomes, and soon you will see how much they all have in common.

For additional help maneuvering the databases, go to iTunesU and download our podcasts with step by step instructions for navigating each database. Simply go to: http://deimos3.apple.com/WebObjects/Core.woa/Browse/mdc-public.3523749442.03523749444.

Tips for Working with JSTOR

In addition to going to certain databases that are subject specific, you also have some databases that will be a collection of subject-specific journals. That means that rather than going into a subject-specific database and typing in keywords and getting results from a variety of journals, you can select from which specific type of journals you would like to see results. JSTOR is one of those databases that is a collection of journals in all different subjects, and you can choose as many or as few as you would like to search for your sources on your topic.

- When you go into JSTOR, as with the other database screens, click on Advanced Search at the top under the "search" tab.

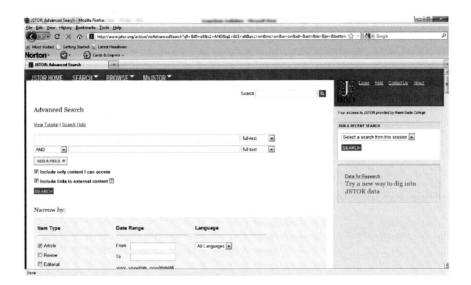

- Keep the search terms on Full Text because you want to ensure that you get results you can read right away in the complete version. It already is set to allow external links to text that is not fully available within JSTOR.

- Under item type, check article, so that you can get full articles as results. (*Note:* Based on previous practice, you may be tempted to click on Review, but do not do that. That does not indicate Peer Reviewed. Most journals in JSTOR are already peer reviewed. The word Review here means book review, and you do not want that as a result because it is not a full source and you do not have the book to which it is referring. Also, depending on your research project, editorials and pamphlets may not be acceptable.)

- Limit your date ranges, just as you have before.

- Once you have done all the familiar steps with searching databases, notice that JSTOR then has a list of Disciplines/Subjects. If you click on the plus sign next to any of those subjects, the database will show you all the journals that JSTOR has related to that subject. Click on any or all of the journals in that subject section in which you would like to search. It is up to you to choose. For your initial search, you will probably want to checkmark the entire subject so the search includes all the journals that JSTOR has.

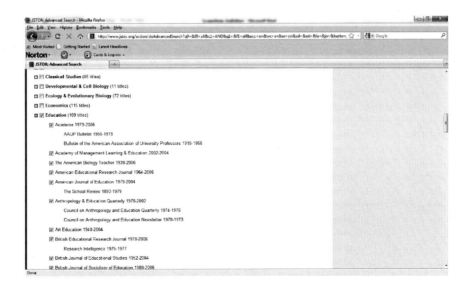

- Then, as before, type in keywords to search for material.
- When you get results from JSTOR, you will find that you can click on the title of any given result to see the full article. (Notice that you also have the title of the journal, the volume and issue number, and the author's name hyperlinked. If you like any article, you can always click on the journal table of contents to see more articles from that same journal, or you can click on all volumes and issues to see more from other editions, or from the results list you can click on the author's name to see if he or she has written anything else on that topic that would be worth using.)

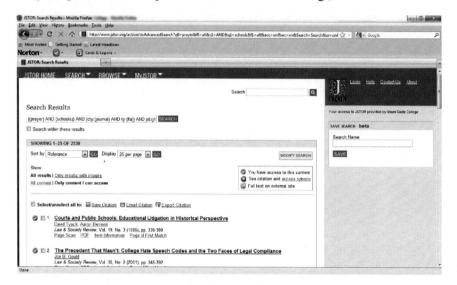

- If you like any result, JSTOR can only e-mail the abstract to you; however, you can print any full article or download (save) any article to a flash drive or computer.

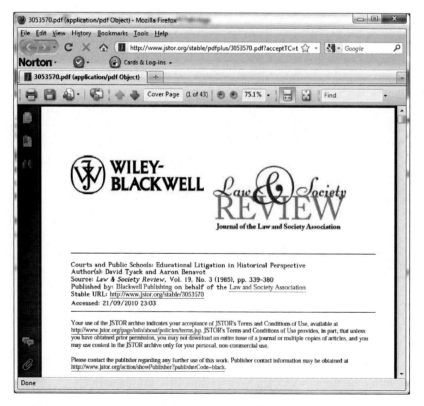

Note: If the result has an arrow next to it instead of a checkmark, it will take you to the 'Find Text' option generated by the SFX service for you to try to track down the article.

For additional help maneuvering the databases, go to iTunesU and download our podcasts with step by step instructions for navigating each database. Simply go to: http://deimos3.apple.com/WebObjects/Core.woa/Browse/mdc-public.3523749442.03523749444.

Tips for Working with NetLibrary

Besides databases that have a collection of articles and journals, there are also databases that are a collection of online books. This is still a growing collection, and there are not nearly as many full-text books online as there are printed books, but this is also an option that you can use if you are trying out a variety of different source types and are interested in working with this type of source. Just remember, some of the complete works are here, some are just the overviews, and some are just the tables of contents; everything is still in progress and more is being added every day.

- When you go into NetLibrary, simply click on Advanced Search, as you have done many times before.

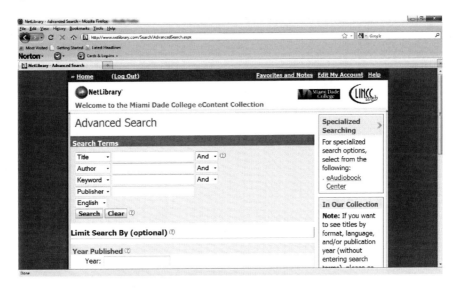

- Once you are on the Advanced Search screen, change the search term from *Title* to *Keyword* so that your results are not so limited.
- Again, you can limit the year range so that you can get current material.
- For format, click on eBooks so that you can get as many full-length results as possible. Then click on Search.
- When you get results in NetLibrary, simply click on the cover of the book that you are interested in.

- Review the table of contents to see if it contains material that you can use for your topic.
- If it is worthwhile, you can then click on the chapter of the book that you think is worthwhile; or, you can print the pages you would like to work with right away. (*Please note:* Be sure to click on e-content details to e-mail the book information to yourself. It is easier to refer back to that than to go in and search for it again in the databases.)

For additional help maneuvering the databases, go to iTunesU and download our podcasts with step by step instructions for navigating each database. Simply go to: http://deimos3.apple.com/WebObjects/Core.woa/Browse/mdc-public.3523749442.03523749444.

Tips for Working with WorldCat (OCLC)

Finally, there are database services that have databases that can give you multiple types of results. These databases can include articles and books, but can also include Web sites, sound recordings, videos, government documents, and so on. WorldCat (OCLC) is one database service that can offer many different types of results, but is especially good for locating books at multiple libraries.

As before, you click on the Advanced Search screen and you can type in keywords. The difference is in the result types. (To make sure you get academic results, please be sure to limit to Not Juvenile and Not Fiction; otherwise, you will get many items that are designed for different levels or for the general public.)

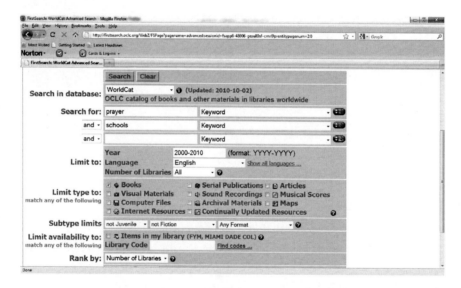

- When you get results in WorldCat, click on the result type you want to look at. For example, you can just click on Books to look at the book listings.
- If you see a result that you like, click on the title for an abstract or table of contents reflecting the book's chapters.
- If you like the book, click on Libraries Worldwide to see the list of libraries that own this book.

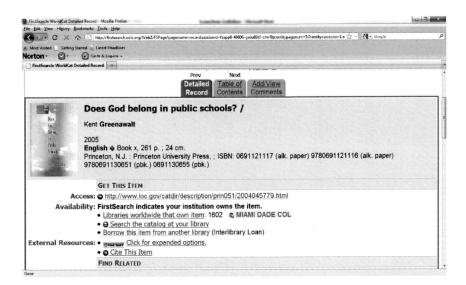

- If you know the book is at a library that you are willing to visit, mark the book by checkmarking next to the number of the result and then click on the library name. Note the call number, location and availability.

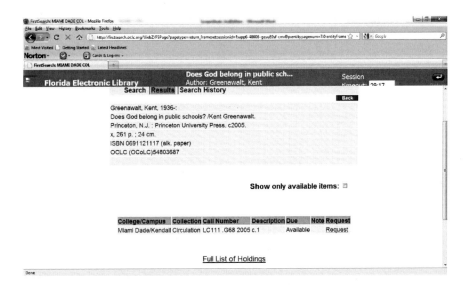

- When you have clicked on all the books that you are interested in, click on Marked Records and you can then print, e-mail, or save the list of books. Remember! These are not links to the books themselves; you must go to the library to get these books as discussed fully in the Print Materials section.
- You can follow the same steps for any of the other tabs such as "Visual," "Articles," "Sound," "Serials," and so on.
- If you click on the "Internet" tab, you will find a lot of links to NetLibrary. (If your library has a link to the NetLibrary database, it will take you straight to the source; otherwise, you will have to just make note of the information and search online for that eBook later.) Or, you may find links to other general Internet Web sites. Unlike a general Google search, the Web sites for these links have been reviewed by media specialists to have been listed in WorldCat and have been deemed academically worthy; so it is worth following these links to see if there is good material related to your topic.

Science Direct

Another database service that you may find very useful is ScienceDirect. As before, you will select it from the list of available databases and then click on 'Connect to Database'. You will notice that the first screen in ScienceDirect allows you to choose the type of science you wish to research on the left-hand side from physical sciences to the social sciences. Depending on your topic, you may narrow down your search this way even before you start.

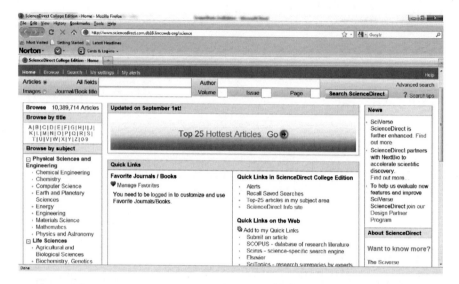

However, if you'd like to keep your options open, simply click on Advanced search in the upper right-hand corner and select 'journals' if you are looking for academic articles before typing in your keywords. This way it will search all the sciences at the same time for the keywords you type in.

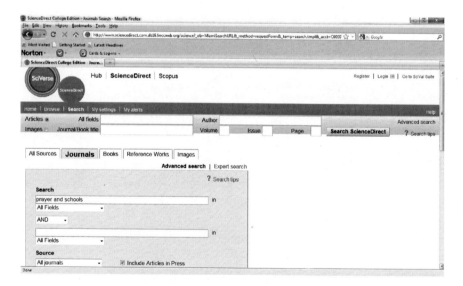

Notice that when you get your list of results, you can refine them by limiting to journals or a specific publication. In addition, underneath each source, it will indicate which results are available full text and which are not. (Note: If you like an article that is not available in full text, you can still click on it to see the abstract and a list of related articles that may have a full text link. Or, if your library has the capability, you can click on the reprint and permissions link underneath the abstract. If your library has a subscription it may lead you to a full text copy much like the SFX service would do.)

For the articles that do have full text available, you'll notice that you can click on the title of the article to see the complete article. (Do not just click on the pdf file itself at first.) Notice that the keywords are highlighted in yellow throughout the article, and there are links to related articles on the right-hand side.

In addition, notice that in the list of references for each article, if ScienceDirect has access to any reference on the list, a link to the full text for that reference is available, directly from within the references section.

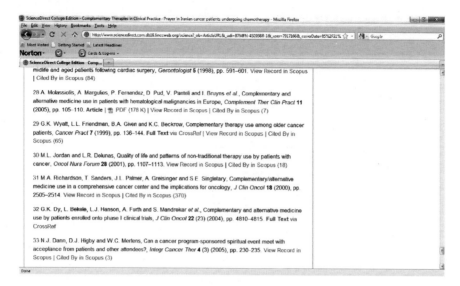

If you decide you like the original article, simply click on the pdf file for the article and print or save the article. (While you can go back to your list of results and mark the records to save the search, it will not save all of the full text of the articles. The saving of that search will simply allow you to go back to that search when you sign in again. Like JSTOR, you will want to either print or the save the articles that you like as you find them.)

Multiple Database Search

Most college and university libraries have the ability to search outside of any specific database service like Wilson, Gale, EBSCO, etc. These multiple database searches vary in quality from school to school, and the main drawback of this type of search is that if you don't know how to navigate inside these different types of databases, when you get results, you may not know where to go to find your source. In other words, we recommend some practice within the different types of databases first before moving on to an external multiple database search. This way you have the skills to find your material easily and quickly.

To begin, you can click on multiple database search (or 360 search or power search . . . these can vary in name). Usually you will be able to select a set of databases by the subject you are researching.

Some may allow you to choose multiple subjects; others may only allow one subject at a time. This would mean searching more than once. (For example, if you're looking at the practice of prayer in schools, it can fall under multiple subjects such as education, social sciences, and legal/government issues. If you're not able to choose multiple subjects at once, don't limit yourself to just one search in education. Do multiple searches.)

Once you type in your keywords, review the results. You'd want them ranked by relevance if possible. You can also narrow down to the most recent results by years or you can narrow further by specific related subjects.

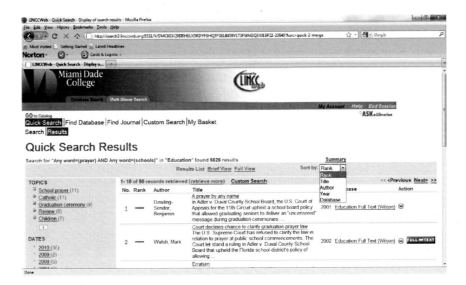

Notice also that most multiple database searches can be narrowed further by authors and specific journals. In addition, some power or multiple database searches will indicate to you that the result is from a peer-reviewed or academic source.

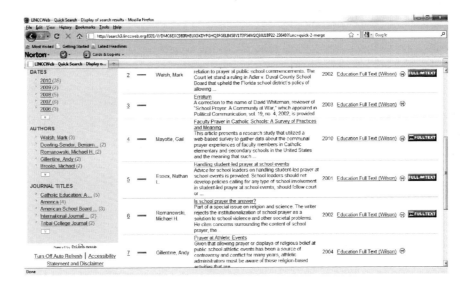

When you click on the full text option, it will then lead you to the 'Go' buttons generated by the SFX service for finding text. As before, follow the search to one of the individual databases (and be certain to note the author and title of what you are looking for; some of the 'Go' buttons may simply lead you to a list of articles) or the general internet for finding that particular article. Note: Sometimes the general internet will have a copy of the article for a cost to you. It is up to you to decide if your research really needs that specific article or if there are other free options that will do just as well. There are millions of articles that are at no cost to you in these databases; unless you are looking for something very particular, there are many more possibilities to explore. We have shown you multitudes of databases, and there are even more than are in this book, but this will definitely help you get the practice you need to become very adept at using any new ones you may encounter.

For additional help maneuvering the databases, go to iTunesU and download our podcasts with step by step instructions for navigating each database. Simply go to: http://deimos3.apple.com/WebObjects/Core.woa/Browse/mdc-public.3523749442.03523749444.

Web Pages

If the visits to all the types of databases are not enough, the Internet is an option; but it is very important that you realize that *not all Web sites are equal.* Remember that the Internet is not regulated; therefore, anyone can create a Web site to say anything. You do not want to build a research paper on just anything. So, at least know the difference between types of Web sites.

A .com or .net Web site is usually a commercial Web site that is either endorsed or advertised on by a commercial product. That usually means it is either selling something or will link you to items for sale. In other words, somebody profits. That can sometimes lead to a bias right from the beginning. That is why these are not usually the best sites to rely upon for sources. However, some .com Web sites, such as major world news Web sites, can have a long history in reliability and validity and would likely be okay. In addition, some research Web sites, like GoogleScholar or FindArticles, are in the process of trying to gather reliable academic sources. Other types of sources are still mixed in, though, and if you are not experienced with academic search results, you may not know the difference. Also, it is so general, as many Internet searches are, that it is best that you try the academic databases first. They are much more subject specific, you can limit results by Peer Reviewed and Full Text most of the time, and you become very experienced with what academic material should sound like. After that experience, you will be able to tell right away when you get results from other sites—just by how they are written—if they are academically worthy or not. So, save the commercial Web sites for a last resort.

The other types of Web sites—.org, .gov, and .edu Web sites (explained in the Identifying Sources section in chapter 1)—are more likely to be Web sites you would want to visit for information that has been verified and is most likely for reliable consumer and public information. (This, of course, excludes user-controlled Web sites like Wikipedia, even if it has a .org in the url address. Being user controlled means that information can be changed by any user at any time. That makes some of the material in Wikipedia unreliable, and you don't want to build your formal academic research paper on that.)

Print Material

Books

Using a book as a source is not uncommon for research papers. But, as previously established, there is not one set "type" of book out there; a book can have multiple authors, it can have editors, it can be part of a series, or so forth. One of the things to always keep in mind is being aware of what type of book you have found. But overall, searching for a book, whatever the type, often follows the same process.

Most students today are of the Internet generation, so you may not even be used to going into libraries anymore; but that does not mean you will not have to at some point. It is important that you are able to navigate them once you are there, so you need to understand what you need to find a book and how you would go about obtaining that book at the library.

Sometimes students will simply go into a library and ask a media specialist for assistance. The media specialist may then direct the student to a certain area of the library where many of those books are found. But, this is not the most efficient method for finding a book; they are there to help you, yes, but you should go in prepared by helping yourself as much as you can first. To make the most of your time, do a little preresearch before going into a library. Take the time to review the library catalog of the library you plan to go to for your topic. As you look at each result, make sure you take note of three important things: *call number, location,* and *availability.* If you do not write these things down or text them to your phone, you may be wasting a trip.

To start a search, you can simply go to the main library Web site and click on Catalog. Then, click on Advanced Search. Then, lower on that screen, limit the format to Books.

Type in the keywords that you would use to search for material related to your topic. When you get results, they will show the book, the call number, and the location.

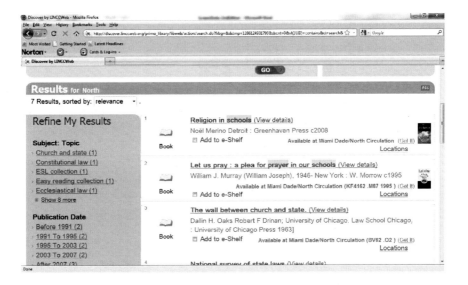

However, it does not always show you if it is available or not. Sometimes it only shows what the library owns and what campus owns it, so if it is checked out, it is not visible. To see if it is available, you would click on the name of the campus that is listed that you plan to visit. It should then show you if it is available or on loan to someone else. (Note: If it states to add to an e-shelf or that it is an e-book, that usually means it can be found in NetLibrary; you can either click on the link and log in with your user ID and password to access the book, or simply note the book information and you can go into NetLibrary later.)

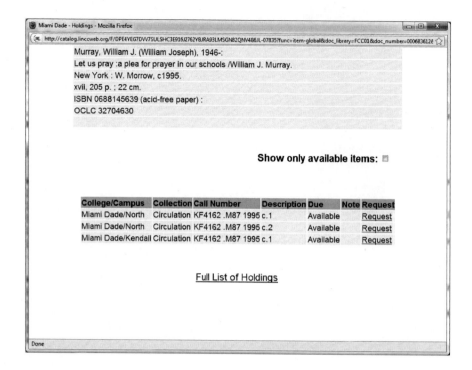

Note: Always have more than one choice when you go to the library! You never know when someone is using the book you planned to check out. Have multiple choices so your odds are high that you will get what you want.

Also, if the book is in fact available, you can request that the book be held if you click on the word Request and put in your student number. Likewise, if you like a book but it is checked out, you can also click on Request and have it sent to your campus. Although it takes a few days, with early planning, you can have a lot of great materials sent to you from other colleges.

Finally, when going into any library, be sure you have written down the exact call number. All of the material in the library is shelved according to that number. Because you limited your search to books, you are looking in the general collection. So, look for the letters first. That will take you to the right section. Then you can follow the numbers.

Please note: If you like a book, and it is not available at your library, you can search for that book title at other universities. Simply search in the university library catalog for the book, and again, check for the location, call number, and availability. Once you do that, go to the local public library and pick up a SEFLIN card. That card, along with your school ID, will allow you to check out material from other participating universities.

Articles

Looking for articles is not really that different from looking for books. Since most of your articles will be full text online from the databases, you can usually get the most contemporary articles online. But, because technology is still not fully caught up with print, you should be aware that for every full-text online article, there are dozens that are not. So follow just a few steps to get to those articles. As with books, you will want to note the call number, location, and availability; but in addition, you should also note the *volume holdings* of the journal that holds the article you are looking for. Again, do not waste a trip to a library thinking that they have the journal article that you want and then find that they have many copies of that journal but not the volume you need.

To get articles that are in print, you can do any of the database searches, but leave off the Full Text option. You can try the SFX option, but for the ones you can't find through those searches either, mark the articles that you like and print out a list of the marked articles. Then you can visit the library catalog again. Only this time, instead of searching by Keyword, search by Title, and type in the name of the journal you want. For example, if you want an article that is from the *American Journal of Psychology,* then type that in. When you get results, as before with books, click on the campus you want to go to in order to see their holdings (that is, what volumes they have).

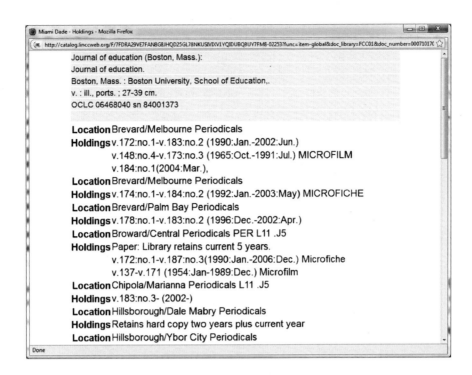

Note: If they have the volume you need that has the article that you want, then write down that it is in the periodicals section, a call number (if they have one), and that it is noncirculating, meaning that it cannot be checked out, so it should be there when you go to search for it. This is what *should* happen. However, as with books, you should have multiple choices when you search for articles, just in case someone is using the volume you need. Also, if your library does not have the volume you need or even the journal you are looking for, you can do this same type of search in another university library catalog. Just note that for universities, the periodicals also use call numbers, just like books. So it may be in the general collection or in recent periodicals, depending on the volume. Again, the call number, location, and availability are key, but so are the volume holdings when it comes to periodicals. (Of course, all of this is to be done only when the university does not have an online link to the journal. Usually if you're on campus, you have access even if you are not a student.)

Finally, because periodicals cannot be checked out, be sure to take money to put on a copy card so you can copy the article on the copy machine or pay for printing from their online journal. If it is your college, then you can just put money on your student ID card. If it is a different university, you can simply buy a guest copy card, usually for a dollar, and then you can put money on that.

Government Documents

The "Government Documents" section is another section of the library that holds a variety of print materials that can be used as sources for research papers. These are not like research articles in the sense that most government documents are primary sources. In other words, instead of reading an article about a court case, you will find a copy of the actual court proceedings. Or, you may find a session of Congress in which a decision was reached about a law. Or, you may find the actual speech given by the Speaker of the House or the President of the United States. These are very interesting sources, and many have been converted to online form. You can find many of these government documents in the FirstSearch (OCLC) databases by clicking on the GPO database. There you will often find links to the actual documents in PDF format. Or, you can search in almost any university library regular catalog and some results will link right to the government document, usually linked to purl.access.gov, or you can go directly to http://www.whitehouse.gov and search the site directly. But, if you are searching a regular library catalog and it does not have that link, then you would follow the same steps to find it as you would for a printed book or article.

When you find a government document through a library catalog or database search that doesn't have a link to the item, then again, do a regular library search; then simply write down the call number and location of the document. Sometimes you will have to check availability as well, but most of the time, government documents cannot be checked out. You will have to copy them on the copy machine. The most important thing to note about government documents, though, is that they are not part of the general collection. In almost every library, the government documents will be in a special section of the library. If you did not look at a library map before visiting your library, simply ask the media specialist and he or she can direct you. Once you have found the government documents, everything is organized by call number, just like the books and periodicals/journals.

Microforms

A final type of source you may be interested in using is a *microform* source. This may be very unfamiliar because most items today are scanned as PDF or HTML files and put online as full text. But, if for some reason you are asked to find material that is from farther back than the last twenty years or so, it is possible that you will find the material in microform.

Two types of microforms are most commonly used: microfilm and microfiche. You may have seen them in the form of small boxes that look like rolls of projector film or that look like small squares of overhead transparency. Their original purpose, much like PDF or HTML files today, was to hold lots of print information in a *micro,* or smaller, form. To view microfilm or microfiche, you need a special machine, which most university libraries today still have.

Note that if you see results in the library catalog that say *microfilm* or *microfiche,* the results will also have a location and call number to note, like everything else, but the microfilm or microfiche will be in a special section of the library, just like government documents. The microform may even be in a neighboring section on the same floor. As long as you have the call number and location, you should be able to pull the right drawer that contains the microfilm or microfiche, and the machines should already be next to them, ready for you to view the articles they contain. In addition, you can usually print pages from the microfilm or microfiche, just as you would if you were making copies on a copy machine. These are perfectly good sources; they just require a little more effort in getting to them.

Success

Overall, finding good, legitimate, and worthwhile academic sources can be accomplished in many ways. There is no shortage of information out there! Learning how to use all of these methods will make you the most experienced and educated of students. Try them all. And believe it not, there are still more methods beyond this and there are still more unique features within each type of database beyond what is listed here. But this is a pretty thorough beginning.

Practice Exercises
Research Scavenger Hunt

Name _____   **Date** _____

Test your search skills by locating information from a variety of sources.

1. A newspaper article published on the day you were born

    Article title: _____

    Article topic: _____

    Newspaper name: _____

    Date of publication: _____

2. A grocery store advertisement from the 1970s

    Date: _____

    Newspaper: _____

    Sale item: _____

    Price of item: _____

3. The first two lines of a book by Bob Woodward

    _____

    _____

    _____

    Book title: _____

    Publisher: _____

    Date: _____

4. A recent article on global warming from an electronic subscription service such as *Gale, EBSCO,* or *WilsonWeb*

    _____

    _____

5. A 2007 article about a presidential candidate from a weekly magazine

   Article title: _____

   Subject: _____

   Magazine title: _____

   Date: _____

6. A journal article about hospice care using the Wilson database

   _____

   _____

7. A pamphlet from the U.S. Department of Immigration and Naturalization

   Title: _____

   Subject: _____

8. A quotation from a program that aired on public television

   _____

   _____

   _____

9. The titles of a social science journal, an education journal, and a medical journal available in your local *university* library

   Social science journal: _____

   Education journal: _____

   Medical journal: _____

10. An article from an online periodical (a magazine or newspaper that publishes online *only*)

   _____

   _____

11. The lead story in today's *New York Times*

   _____

   _____

Identifying Newspaper Names

Name _____   **Date** _____

A list of American and international cities follows. Use the Internet to find the name of each city's major newspaper.

New York _____

Los Angeles _____

Chicago _____

San Francisco _____

Dallas _____

Kansas City _____

Newark _____

Miami _____

Boston _____

Edinburgh _____

London _____

Dublin _____

Sydney _____

Montreal _____

Toronto _____

Barbados _____

Nassau _____

Chapter 3

Incorporating Material from Sources

Reading and Highlighting

When you read your articles, highlight important pieces of information, but be selective. Remember to limit your highlighting to the following.

- Facts
- Statistics
- Definitions
- Significant data
- Important ideas
- Critical examples

Do not highlight entire paragraphs. Extract only specific information within a paragraph. In the course of reading an article, you might find the number of relevant sections varies. In one article, you might find only one line that suits your research focus. In another, you might highlight in six different areas.

Each time you highlight a particular passage or line, make a note in the margin that identifies the specific topic of that passage. For example, if you are reading an article on hybrid cars, you might find a passage that discusses the miles per gallon that a Honda Fit gets. In the margin, you might use the key words or label "fuel economy." Later in the same article, you might read a sentence about the low emissions of hybrid vehicles. A good margin label or key word would be, naturally, "emissions." In another article, you may find information about the Toyota Prius getting up to fifty miles per gallon. In the margin, you would write the key words or label "fuel efficiency." In another article, you might read about the Ford Explorer Hybrid and the hybrid Saturn Vue. You may write as your topic label "U.S. hybrid production" or "American hybrids."

Follow these steps with all of your articles. A key word or topic label should be brief, no more than two or three words that serve as an identifier. The label should be an accurate reflection of the information in the passage. You will need these specific and precise key words to write your note cards. By the time you finish reading and highlighting six or seven articles, you should have close to thirty highlighted areas ready to be transferred to note cards.

Bibliography Cards

Recording Your Sources: Writing Bibliography Cards

Organization is the key to conducting research and preparing a research paper. That means that you keep track of every relevant source you find as you search for information and write down all the publication information so you will be ready to prepare the works cited page on your paper. To do this, you will need a stack of blank index cards. For each source you find, copy the necessary information onto an index card exactly the way the MLA requires. See Chapter 5 of this text or your MLA Handbook for more information. How do you know which information is necessary? How do you determine where to write the volume number or whether you should include it at all? The only way to record bibliographical information correctly is by consulting the MLA section of your handbook (either the hard copy or its online version).

First, you need to identify the type of source you have. It could be a weekly magazine, a daily newspaper, an article on a Web site, a documentary you saw on the History Channel, or so forth. Once you establish the source type, find the directions for that particular works cited entry. Most handbooks provide a numbered list of source types to make navigating the guide easier. For example, if you look in the MLA documentation section of the *Bedford Handbook* (eighth edition), you will find such a list on page 530–531.

Suppose you have an editorial in a newspaper. Locate the heading "Articles in Periodicals" (in the *Bedford Handbook*) and you will find that number 31, "editorial or other unsigned article," leads you to page 545. On page 545, you will find the precise format for recording the publication information as it will eventually appear in your paper's works cited page.

If you have trouble identifying and locating the format for one of your sources, ask your instructor for assistance. Some handbooks have not yet incorporated methods for listing newer types of online sources like podcasts and blogs.

Most of your materials will come from periodicals, but you might become frustrated trying to figure out whether the periodical is a newspaper, a journal, or a magazine. Beyond that, even if you do determine that your source is a magazine, you will need to determine whether it is a weekly or monthly magazine because the information required is different for each. For instance, a monthly magazine will have only the month and the year listed, and a weekly magazine will have the exact date of publication. The MLA asks you to format your works cited entries accordingly. Remember that most of this material was covered in the Chapter 1 section *Identifying Sources.*

Practice Recording Bibliographical Information

Name _____ **Date** _____

Write in the requested information for each of the source types below. When you have finished, you will learn how to transfer the information to index cards to create your bibliography cards.

You will need

Blank index cards
Copies of articles on your topic
Your handbook or MLA guide

In the space provided, extract the necessary publication information from your sources as identified. Once you have done this, you can transfer the information and format your bibliography cards properly.

- Book

    Author(s):

    Book title:

    City of publication:

    Publisher:

    Date:

    Medium:

- Monthly magazine

    Author(s):

    Article title:

    Magazine title:

    Date:

    Page numbers:

    Medium:

- Journal Article

    Author(s):

    Article title:

    Journal title:

    Volume number:

Issue number:

Date or season:

Page numbers:

Medium:

- Entire Web site

  Author (if any):

  Web site title:

  Sponsor of site:

  Date updated:

  Medium:

  Date you accessed the information:

  *Web address:

  *Note: if your instructor requires this, enclose it in angle brackets at the end of the entry.

- Newspaper

  Author(s) (if any):

  Article title:

  Newspaper title:

  Date:

  Name of edition (if any):

  Page:

  Medium:

- Work from a subscription service such as Gale or EBSCO

  Author(s):

  Article title:

  Periodical title:

  Volume/issue number(s):

  Publication date:

  Page numbers (n. pag. if there are none)

  Name of database:

  Medium:

  Date you accessed source:

Just record the information exactly the way the Modern Language Association (MLA) asks you to, remembering the following key points.

- The first line goes all the way to the left. Only the lines that follow get indented.

  It should look like this.

  _____

     _____

     _____

- Punctuation counts! If the MLA puts a period after the article title, make sure you put a period after the article title. If the MLA says a magazine title is underlined or italicized, make sure you do not enclose it in quotation marks. Make sure you put a period at the end of each entry.
- Pay attention to the way authors' names are listed. When a source lists more than one author, you need to record those names in a very particular order as per MLA directions. Read your handbook closely!
- Pay attention to the format for dates, including abbreviations of months. Additional information and visuals for MLA format can be found in Chapter 5 and the handbook.

A sample bibliography card for a weekly magazine article follows.

Klein, Joe. "The Race Goes On." *Time.* 17 March 2008: 25-27.

In the space below, write a sample bibliography card.

Identifying Bibliography Card Errors

Name _____   **Date** _____

Identify the errors in the following bibliography cards.

> David Westin. "The Truth about TV News." *America Now:*
> *Readings from Recent Periodicals.* Ed. Robert Atwan.
> Boston/New York: *Bedford/St.* Martins, 2007. 343-347.

> Westin, David. <u>The Truth about TV News</u>. "America Now:
> Readings from Recent Periodicals". Ed. Robert Atwan.
> Boston/New York: *Bedford/St.* Martins, 2007. 343-347.

> David Westin. "The Truth about TV News." *America Now:*
> *Readings from Recent Periodicals.* Ed. Robert Atwan. Boston/New York: *Bedford/St.*
> Martins, 2007. 343-347.

Westin, David.. "The Truth about TV News." *America Now: Readings from Recent Periodicals*. Ed. Robert Atwan. Boston/New York: *Bedford/St.* Martins, 2007. Pgs.343-347.

Westin, David. "The Truth about TV News," *America Now: Readings from Recent Periodicals* Robert Atwan, Ed.. Boston/New York: *Bedford/St.* Martins, 2007. 343-347.

Note Card Forms

At this point in the process, you are ready to transfer the highlighted information from your articles to blank index cards; these become what we call "note cards." Every highlighted area will become a separate note card. If you read an article and highlighted five places within the article, you will write five note cards for that article. If you read a four-page article and found only one sentence useful enough to highlight, then that article will generate only one note card. You will transfer only one piece of information per card; it can be a phrase, a sentence, or a group of sentences from the same paragraph. If you read significant material in one paragraph and then two paragraphs later you find more information, that will be transferred to a new index card.

Note Card Format

Every note card has three parts:

- The topic label (the key words you wrote in the article margin)
- The author's last name and the page number
- The information itself

First, write the topic label on the top of your card. This will identify your topic. In the course of your reading many articles, you will find yourself writing a few note cards on that same topic. Why? Because the notes from the card will become supporting details in your paragraph, and the more supporting details and examples you offer your reader, the more convincing your paper will be.

Next, be sure to include the author's name and the page number. If your source is an unauthored Web site, use the first few words of the title instead of the author and page number. More information on this can be found in your handbook or Chapter 5, where we discuss the specifics of MLA in-text citations.

Finally, copy the information onto the card. If you are copying word for word (quoting the original source directly), do not make any changes and make sure you enclose all the information within quotation marks. If you are paraphrasing, interpret and transfer the information very carefully.

Types of Note Cards

Note cards all serve the same purpose—to provide you with the specific and organized information you need to draft your paper—but they can be divided into four types: direct quotation, paraphrase, combination, and summary.

Direct Quotation

Using *direct quotation,* you write down word for word what you read in your source. Do not change anything, not a comma, not a word, not a space. **Make sure you enclose the words in quotation marks to indicate direct quotation.** You are not looking for things other people said in the article. *You* are the person quoting the article. When you take information word for word, you are quoting your source. You enclose what you have taken in quotation marks to indicate to the reader that these words were exactly as you found them in the article.

Paraphrase

Paraphrase is the *danger* zone, so pay attention. When you use a source's ideas but change the words, you paraphrase. Paraphrase is a required research skill; most of your research paper will include paraphrased material rather than direct quotations.

You do not enclose paraphrases in quotation marks. Even though the words are your own, the ideas belong to someone else, and you must properly credit the source as you do when you directly quote. You identify the source on the note card and, of course, eventually within the paper itself. Paraphrase requires two key components: first, you must change the words; and second, you must change the sentence structure so it does not resemble the original. One final point is that you must not use any form of the original word as well. That means if the original passage uses the word "responsible," you cannot use the word "responsibility." An appropriate alternative would be "dependability." This skill requires practice.

Combination

A *combination* note card gives you the best of both options. Sometimes you need to use a particular phrase from the original passage because changing it would alter the meaning or tone, but you do not need to copy the entire sentence or passage. In that case, you can paraphrase most of the material and enclose the few words directly from the source in quotation marks. You are combining your words with the author's. This method allows you to "pick and choose" and smoothly integrate the original into your own writing.

Summary

A *summary* note is what it says it is: a summary. If you read a study or an article and would like to reference its main points without quoting or paraphrasing very specific areas, you can summarize it. Remember to include a signal phrase or explanation of the study.

Setup

No matter what type of card you write, it must contain the standard requirements: the topic label and the author's last name and the page number on which that passage appeared. If your article has no author, use the first few words of the title in quotation marks. If it has two authors, use both last names connected by *and.* If it has no page number, you are not required to provide one. According to MLA, you would not need to include one. Again, more specifics on this and other MLA requirements are provided in your handbook and Chapter 5.

Set up your cards carefully so you can read the label and the author information. Many people prefer putting the label on the top left and the author's name and the page number on the top right. Other people prefer putting the author's name and the page number below the other recorded information on the note card. Do what works for you or, better yet, what your professor suggests.

Writing Note Cards

The bulk of your final research paper comes from the notes you take as you read through your sources; you do not draft your paper directly from the articles. To make the process manageable, the MLA developed an organized system of note taking wherein you write each piece of useful information on a separate index card, label it, and include the source. By the time you finish the note taking phase of the project, you will have anywhere from twenty to forty note cards with facts, figures, and significant details to support a six- to ten-page paper.

When reading the articles you retrieve, you need to have a highlighter in your hand so you are ready to identify the important elements you wish to transfer to the index cards. To know what to extract from the articles, use the following list as a guide.

- *Pertinent information.* Write down any information *directly related* to your chosen topic.
- *Statistic and numerical data.* Numbers often speak louder than words. Pertinent numerical data lend credibility to your paper.
- *Significant facts.* Sometimes you will need to write down historical facts or background information. If you are in doubt of a fact's value, write it down anyway—better safe than sorry.
- *Notable points.* Write down key points and arguments.
- *Unique or significant statements.* If you come across a pivotal, thought-provoking, or eloquently worded statement, use it. Remember to include a signal phrase to identify the source.
- *Exceptions and counterarguments.* Be prepared to acknowledge and refute the opposition where applicable. Hiding from opposing viewpoints will not strengthen your position.

Note how the student transferred the information from the original source to her note card and finally into a paragraph in her research paper.

Original Source

Miller, Elizabeth. "The Question of Immortality: Vampires, Count Dracula, and Vlad the Impaler."
    Journal of Dracula Studies 4 (2002) n. pag.

The Question of Immortality:
Vampires, Count Dracula, and Vlad the Impaler
Elizabeth Miller

[Elizabeth Miller has published and lectured widely. She is currently working on a volume on Dracula for the Dictionary of Literary Biography. This essay was a paper given at the TSD Symposium in Romania in 2002.]

What constitutes immortality? There are essentially two definitions: first, "endless life, the condition of living forever, of never dying"; and secondly, "fame that is likely to last forever." When applied to the three entities that are the subject of this paper—the vampire, the Count Dracula of Bram Stoker's novel, and the historical personage whose nickname "Dracula" Stoker borrowed—both definitions raise problematic issues.

Immortality is often cited as one of the chief characteristics of the vampire. Indeed, today it can account to a great extent for the tremendous appeal of the vampire in western popular culture, not only fulfilling (albeit a fictional universe) the human yearning for eternal life, but filling a void created by skepticism about and even abandonment of traditional religious faith. Furthermore, for many, the lure of the vampire lies in the ideal of eternal youth. But these paradigms are more of a modern (or even postmodern) construct than an essential part of either folklore or traditional vampire literature.

Student's Note Card

Immortality	Miller 1
"Immortality is often cited as one of the chief characteristics of the vampire."	

Now notice how the student integrates the material from her note card into her paragraph as she writes.

Trujillo 1

Ashley Trujillo

Professor Shaw

ENC 1102H

23 April 2010

Sample Paragraph-Integrating Sources

The first main idea that is emphasized in the life of Dracula and the life of Jesus is immortality. What is the exact definition of immortality? What does it mean for one to be immortal? Immortality means to have an unending existence. In Dracula's world, the immortal being roams around this earth seeking to devour the innocent. Immortality is often noted as "one of the chief characteristics of the vampire" (Miller 1). Vampires can live forever, or until someone kills them. One character Mina, writes about her experience. ". . . The knife went through it, empty as the air" (Stoker 80). This novel affirms that immortality can be possible in the earth and that these immortals can live with the mortals. Dracula walks the earth day and night with no end of his life coming near and his only concern is to not be stabbed. Other than that, he is an immortal being who has the control to do as he pleases.

Practice Writing Note Cards

Name _____   **Date** _____

Select a highlighted passage from one of your research articles. Then transfer the information to note cards, using the same information to write three different forms of notes. Proficiency in research means using various methods of note taking.

Direct Quotation

Topic Label	Author and Page Number

Paraphrase

Topic Label	Author and Page Number

Combination

Topic Label	Author and Page Number

Direct Quotation

Topic Label	Author and Page Number

Paraphrase

Topic Label	Author and Page Number

Combination

Topic Label	Author and Page Number

Paraphrasing Extracted Information

Paraphrasing correctly is a required research skill that demands full attention and practice. When you are responsible for conveying someone else's intention, you are bound by ethics to be faithful. Successful paraphrasing involves three key skills:

Understanding

Interpreting objectively

Rephrasing

The third of these must honor the meaning of the original.

Most American adults remember former President Clinton's involvement in a sexual scandal with a White House Intern, but even more than the episode itself is the memorable line most frequently attributed to the president as he denied involvement with Monica Lewinsky.

"I did not have sexual relations with that woman, Miss Lewinsky."

Unfortunately, the press chose to cut off the end of the quotation, which became internationally famous as "I did not have sexual relations with that woman." By ending with "that woman," the statement strongly suggests disrespect for Monica Lewinksy, who does not appear to merit a name when, in fact, President Clinton did respectfully acknowledge her. Most media outlets did record the original quotation, yet they did not publicize it; the words "Miss Lewinsky" trailed off into public oblivion, and people remember only what was played and replayed on radio and television around the country.

If we can make such errors when we quote someone, imagine how many errors we can make when we paraphrase! With one simple word or the omission of one simple word, we can change the entire meaning of an original sentence. When we paraphrase, we need to maintain the integrity of the original quotation and still change the words and sentence structure, not an easy task for a beginning writer.

Using Signal Phrases

A signal phrase prepares your reader for a quotation or paraphrase. It lets the reader know that you, as the writer, are about to use the work or ideas you found during your research. Signal phrases work much like transitions in a regular essay; they ease the movement from your own words to the borrowed material. When you include a quotation without a signal phrase, it seems as if it just floated into your paper or was just randomly "dropped" there—hence, the term *dropped quotation*. Dropped quotations are inappropriate for two reasons: (1) they are confusing to the reader; and (2) they do not provide required, immediate identification of their source.

A common weakness in research writing is a student's dependence upon the same worn out and boring signal phrases *says, states,* or *writes.* Relying on these three words during the course of a ten-page paper breeds monotony. It is much more effective (and impressive) to use signal phrases with particular connotations and meanings. Review the following list.

- To indicate neutrality: *writes, states, reports, observes, points out, notes*
- To show argument: *argues, claims, contends, maintains, believes, insists*
- To indicate support: *concurs, agrees, endorses*
- To highlight a particular point: *emphasizes, underscores*
- To suggest: *suggests, implies*
- To indicate example: *illustrates, proves, supports, adds, explains*
- To indicate acceptance: *acknowledges, understands, admits, grants, confirms*
- To prepare a counterargument: *denies, rejects, refutes, responds, answers, disputes*

Attempts at Paraphrasing

Here are some student attempts—some of them quite humorous—to paraphrase Bill Clinton's original statement. The words making each attempt unsuccessful are italicized. See if you can explain why these words render the paraphrase incorrect. Remember, an incorrect paraphrase will result in plagiarism. Only a few of these would actually be acceptable paraphrases.

Bill Clinton stated that he and Monica Lewinsky *didn't have* sex.

According to Bill Clinton, he *did not have sexual* intercourse with Monica Lewinsky.

It was denied by Bill Clinton that he had *sexual relations* with Monica Lewinsky.

Bill Clinton *insisted* that he *did not have sexual* intercourse with Monica Lewinsky.

Bill Clinton said that he and Monica Lewinsky never had sex.

Bill Clinton *affirmed* that Monica Lewinsky and *him* did not have *any* sexual intercourse.

Bill Clinton declared that he did not sleep with Monica Lewinsky.

Bill Clinton completely denied having *been* involved in any kind of *sexual relations* with this particular woman.

Bill Clinton *denied the accusations of adultery.*

Bill Clinton said he did not have a *physical or intimate* relationship with Monica Lewinsky.

Bill Clinton said that sex was never a part of his and Monica Lewinsky's *professional interactiveness.*

Bill Clinton denied sexual involvement with Monica Lewinsky.

Bill Clinton denied committing adultery with Miss Lewinsky.

Bill Clinton denied being involved in adultery with Miss Lewinsky.

Bill Clinton denied accusations of having sexual intercourse with Monica Lewinsky.

Bill Clinton said that sex never occurred between him and Monica Lewinsky.

Bill Clinton denied engaging in sexual intercourse with Monica Lewinsky.

Bill Clinton said, "I did not have sex with that woman."

Bill Clinton said, "I did not remember that I knew that woman sexually."

Some of the students omitted the signal phrase and were making confessions themselves. These attempts will illustrate the importance of a signal phrase.

That woman and I did not have any *physical contact.*

It is untrue that I've had a sexual affair with that lady.

Ms. Lewinsky and I have not fooled around.

Bill Clinton stated that he was not intimate with *that woman.*

There were not any intimate interactions between me and that significant other.

I didn't have intimate relations with that lady.

Bill Clinton denied having intercourse with Monica Lewinsky.

That lady was not intimately involved with me.

There was no hibbity dibbity between this person and I.

Exercise: How many different ways can you successfully paraphrase the original?

Extracting and Using Material from Sources

Once you locate a useful article, print it out and record the publication information. When you read the article select only the most important piece(s) of information to frame in your own paragraph. Remember to introduce it with the proper signal phrase.

Academic Search Complete (EBSCO)

Title:	Emotions in the Story of an Hour.
Author:	Jamil, S. Selina
Add.Author / Editor:	Jamil, S. Selina
Citation:	Explicator Spring 2009, Vol. 67 Issue 3, p215–220
Year:	2009

Note the following excerpt from S. Selina Jamil's critique of Kate Chopin's "The Story of an Hour" as it appeared in the Spring 2009 issue of *The Explicator:*

> As Chopin demonstrates, this heightened consciousness comes to the protagonist because of her awakened emotions. Revealing her own dynamic and avant-garde understanding, Chopin rejects the tradition of attributing supremacy to the faculty of reason in the act of perception, and she attributes it instead to the faculty of emotions. When she hears the news of her husband's death, **Mrs. Mallard's obliviousness to the beauty of life breaks down under the powerful impact of emotion.** Until this moment, **Mrs. Mallard hardly thinks it worthwhile to continue her existence;** as the narrator of the story says, "It was only yesterday [Mrs. Mallard] had thought with a shudder that life might be long" (194).

Now observe how ENC 1102 student, Alexis Padron, correctly used the most pertinent portion of that article to support her own analysis in the following example.

Alexis Padron

ENC1102MWF

"The Story of an Hour"

Submitted: May 21, 2010, 09:44:27 AM EDT

Score: 5 out of 6

Question:

Essay:

Till Death Do Us Part

Oh the sweet joy death has brought Mrs. Mallard in "The Story of an Hour". This story by Kate Chopin shows the lack of independence women had in the 1800's. When a woman with a weak heart is told her husband was killed in a train accident, she is sad at first. Then the realization that "There would be no one to live for during those coming years; she would live for herself." begins to set in. The thought new life, alone, fills her with joy. Yet, this joy is short lived. As she is walking down the stairs, her husband walks through the door. When she realizes her newly found freedom is now gone, her weak heart gives out, and she dies of a heart attack. Everyone around her is convinced she dies of happiness when she sees that her husband is alive. In reality, she dies of sadness when she realizes that she would not be free at all. Kate Chopin uses irony to show that in the 1800's some women felt chained in their marriages, but could do little about it.

What if you were stuck with someone you no longer wanted to be with for another 20 or 30 years? Mrs. Mallard loved her husband, but this doesn't mean she was in love with him. Today, it's as simple as filling some paper works, deciding who gets what, and moving on. In the 1800's, it was a binding commitment that was only broken through death. Mrs. Mallard wasn't an evil woman who wished death upon her husband. "She wept at once" when she learned of her husband's death. She retreated to her room, and didn't want to come out. Yet, sitting there alone made her realize something. Even though "she was striving to beat it back", she couldn't help but get excited that never had to worry about him again.

Mrs. Mallard was now free. She was free to do as she pleased. She didn't have a husband to tell her what to do. As S. Selina Jamil points out, "Mrs. Mallard's obliviousness to the beauty of life breaks down under the powerful impact of emotion." She also wouldn't be looked down upon, because she was a widow, not an adulterer. This new freedom brought joy to her weak heart. Mrs. Mallard was now young and free. The clearing of the sky outside and the singing of the birds made the realization that she was free all more real. The thought of an entire life of freedom pushes away the thoughts that her husband has even died.

Thinking of many days spent alone and free makes her wish for a long life. This is a new wish for her. Just the day before, a thought of a long life made her sad because the long life would be spent trapped. Now this new life would be all hers and she wants it to last! Mrs. Mallard is now ready to face the world, the new world she is excited to live in. This happiness is about to come to a tragic end. The ideas she had had about freedom are about to come crashing down. Her husband came walking through the door as she was walking down the stairs. He wasn't on the train. Oh the tragic luck of him not being on that train. Her heart gives out. The pain of having this freedom so suddenly and having it taken away just as suddenly was too much on her weak heart.

Kate Chopin used irony in this story to show that Mrs. Mallard was unhappy in her marriage. All the people around her thought her heart gave out from shear joy, but it is made clear that the sadness of realizing her new freedom was gone was too much for her to handle. She never thought she'd be free. Yet, for it to come and go so quickly was tragic. This story is a great depiction of what marriage was like in the 1800's. Many women craved the freedom they knew they'd never achieve. As S. Selina Jamil observes, "Mrs. Mallard hardly thinks it's worthwhile to continue her existence." while she was under the binds of her marriage. Since she is under those binds again, her own death becomes her new way of achieving freedom.

Chopin, Kate. "The Story of an Hour." Living Literature: An Introduction to Poetry, Fiction, and Drama. Ed. John C. Brereton. New York: Pearson Longman, 2008.16–18. Print.

Jamil, S. Selina. "Emotions in the Story of an Hour." The Explicator 67.3 (2009): 215–220. Print.

Just remember that extracting information from sources and integrating it into your own essays and research papers takes time and practice, but the more effort you put in to learning how to do it correctly, the better you will become at demonstrating your research and writing skills.

Chapter 4

Drafting
the Research Paper

Plagiarism

Defining and Avoiding Plagiarism

Whenever you begin research projects, you will undoubtedly hear the word *plagiarism* in class lectures and instruction. Chances are you have heard this word in previous research assignments as well, but chances are equally strong that you have not been given a clear definition and thus have actually been guilty of plagiarism in your past assignments. Perhaps you have read information in a book, encyclopedia, or article; changed it into your own words; and presented it to your teacher with a "Bibliography" or "Works Cited" page and considered your work acceptable. The bad news is that if you have done this, you have plagiarized. In fact, you have probably plagiarized most if not all of the research papers you submitted in classes before taking a college-level research course. To prevent a recurrence of this, you must first understand plagiarism. *Plagiarism* is the act of plagiarizing. *Merriam-Webster's Collegiate Dictionary, Eleventh Edition,* defines *plagiarize* as follows.

1. to steal and pass off (the ideas or words of another) as one's own . . .
2. to commit literary theft: present as new or original an idea or product derived from an existing source

We cannot stress strongly enough the necessity for you to cite—to identify—the source of every idea, piece of information, and word you use if it is not 100 percent your own. Many students worry that citing so many sources in a paper makes the work appear as if it is a mere conglomeration of other people's work. That is partially true; however, the scholar demonstrates academic prowess by reading, using, and commenting further upon the researched material. When writing the research paper, it is not enough to "toss in" the material you find in your searches; you add to that material with your explanations, additional examples, and commentary.

Plagiarism means using another's *words or ideas* as your own without giving proper credit within the paper. This means that even if you rephrase an idea you read in a source or heard in the media, that is, even if it is completely in your own words, you *must still give proper credit to the original source.* If the idea did not come to you in a dream, frenzy of inspiration, or as a divine whisper from some angelic or extraterrestrial source, regardless of the words you assemble to present that idea, you must indicate its origin as soon as you use it. This means that when you put something into your own words, you must immediately follow it with a citation in parentheses. A citation is the method of telling the reader where you found the information as soon as you use that information. In parentheses, the citation simply identifies the author's last name and the page number on which the information appeared. If there is no author, the citation includes part of the article title. If it is an Internet source without a page number, the MLA has a method of citing that as well. Consult your handbook or your instructor for more examples.

Plagiarism is a crime. Lifting another person's ideas is theft—and therefore a criminal act. If you owned a car dealership and someone took a car from the showroom without your permission, it would be considered theft; someone would have unlawfully stolen your product, the means by which you make a living. Taking a writer's words or ideas without properly crediting him or her is the research equivalent. You are stealing the writer's product, the means by which that person earns his or her livelihood.

The penalty for plagiarism in a research course ranges from failing the paper to failing the course. In some institutions, expulsion is the ultimate consequence of plagiarism. Be smart and play it safe. Develop the habit of crediting your source in two ways (or both).

1. In-text citation: in parentheses, identifying the author and page number immediately following your use of the borrowed information
2. Signal phrase: one way of introducing the information by attributing it to its source (see the section on signal phrases for examples)

Note: When you name the author in a signal phrase, you include only the page number in the parenthetical citation. According to MLA, you would not need to include one if you do not have the original page numbers.

When in doubt, *cite!* You will not get a failing grade on a paper for citing a source when it is not necessary, but you are likely to get a failing grade when you omit the citations.

Plagiarism is not limited to unethical borrowing of another writer's material. You are also guilty of plagiarism if you have too much help from someone in writing your paper or you borrow from yourself, that is, if you use material you have used in another essay or a research paper you wrote for another class at another time. The research paper you present to your professor should be completely yours and *new.*

What do you not have to cite? The rule is, anything that is common knowledge need not be cited. A historical fact recognized by the majority of people would not need citation; for example, "The United States declared its independence from Britain on July 4, 1776" would not need to be cited. However, "we hold these truths to be self-evident, that all men are created equal" should be attributed to Thomas Jefferson, who penned the Declaration of Independence.

Plagiarism in the Internet Age

Proceed with caution! The information age has paved the way to the Internet age, which makes available to the average person an unprecedented supply of journals, newspapers, articles, reference books, pamphlets, Web sites, and personal blogs. This information may be free of charge, but it is definitely not free to use without properly crediting the source. Finding an article on the Internet does not give you license to lift that information and insert it into your paper. You are still bound by copyright laws, as well as academic ethics, and must provide the source of information within the paper just as you do with print material.

Oh, and about those *"THOUSANDS OF FREE ESSAYS ON ANY SUBJECT!"* Web sites—understand that if you found them, your professors are certainly familiar with them, too. Besides, this research paper you are writing is not a single paper but a six- to eight-week project completed in small, sequential steps. Any paper you buy on the Internet will have to be dismantled; you will need to locate and print all of the original sources of information cited in those papers; you will need to prepare bibliography and note cards and follow every step of the research process to complete your project successfully, so why unnecessarily invest financially in fraud and compromise your ethics? Once you complete the research process authentically, you will not only enjoy a sense of personal gratification but will be equipped to confront the academic challenges that await you in your upper-level courses.

The professors grading your papers during and after a basic research course do not accept the excuse of "accidental plagiarism." If you are in a college English Composition class, you have been taught the definition of plagiarism. If you are reading this sentence, you can no longer claim ignorance as an excuse. To see what (or whether something) in your paper must be cited, use the following guide.

Have I taken this directly from the original source? If you answer yes, then you must enclose it in quotation marks and cite it in parentheses within the paper.

Have I omitted any words? If you answer yes, pay very close attention. Changing one or two words does not free you from plagiarism. If the surrounding words are the same, you are still a plagiarist.

Have I changed all the word forms? For example, if the original article uses the word *responsible* and you use the word *responsibility,* you are still plagiarizing. You must change words completely.

Have I changed the sentence structure? Not only must you change the words, you must change the sentence structure, reconstructing the entire sentence. It should not be like the original at all.

The Internet hosts many Web sites devoted to understanding and avoiding plagiarism. We strongly recommend the following sites.

http://www.indiana.edu/%7Ewts/pamphlets/plagiarism.shtml

Indiana University, Bloomington, has compiled a very comprehensive Web site on student plagiarism with detailed examples and information. It includes clear definitions, examples, and tips on avoiding plagiarism.

http://web.uflib.ufl.edu/msl/subjects/Physics/StudentPlagiarism.html

The University of Florida library offers a plagiarism Web site with links to many other useful Internet resources.

http://owl.english.purdue.edu/owl/resource/589/01/

There are few writing sites that are as comprehensive and thorough in writing as the Purdue Online Writing Lab (OWL). This site offers an overview of plagiarism, a few exercises, and several examples and guidelines for documentation.

Plagiarism and Paraphrase Exercises

Name _____   **Date** _____

The most challenging task for a student beginning research is avoiding what can be termed "unintentional plagiarism." Changing the words of the original is challenging enough, but changing the sentence structure requires particular skill. Some famous historical quotations follow. For each statement, change both the words and the sentence structure so that they retain the intended message but sound completely different. Be sure to use a signal phrase before your revision.

"All of us might wish at times that we lived in a more tranquil world, but we don't. And if our times are difficult and perplexing, so are they challenging and filled with opportunity."—Robert Kennedy

_____

_____

_____

_____

_____

_____

_____

"The future belongs to those who prepare for it today."—Malcolm X

_____

_____

_____

_____

_____

_____

_____

"You've got to learn to survive a defeat. That's when you develop character."—Richard M. Nixon

_____

_____

_____

_____

_____

_____

_____

"The great danger for family life, in the midst of any society whose idols are pleasure, comfort and independence, lies in the fact that people close their hearts and become selfish."—Pope John Paul II

_____

_____

_____

_____

_____

_____

_____

Yet *Another* Plagiarism Exercise

Name _____   **Date** _____

Copy a passage from one of your research articles here. Select about four or five sentences.

_____

_____

_____

_____

_____

Now, in your own words, write a brief paragraph that includes only one piece of information from the passage you selected. Introduce it properly and cite it parenthetically.

_____

_____

_____

_____

_____

Next, extract a word-for-word statement from that passage. Include it in your own paragraph, both introducing and parenthetically citing it correctly.

_____

_____

_____

_____

_____

Thesis Statement

Your thesis statement will be a comprehensive statement that covers the major points your paper addresses. While it does not include specific detail, it must be specific enough to identify the issues you will discuss in the body of the paper. Remember, the thesis is your promise to the reader that your paper will cover these issues. As in all essay writing, the thesis statement is not going to be a fact but a well-developed one-sentence summary of your information.

We first reinforce what *not* to do.

1. Do not announce, "The paper that follows will explore hybrid technology in the auto industry."
2. Do not quote. Using someone else's words identifies you as a writer incapable of formulating your own thoughts and articulating them clearly.
3. Do not be overly broad or general. "Censorship is a problem in a free society."
4. Do not be excessively narrow or factual. *"The Catcher in the Rye* was censored when it was first published."

Now we explore methods of creating successful thesis statements.

Review your note cards. Consider all the labels. List those topics here.

_____

_____

Your paper addresses all of the topics you just listed. In a few words, summarize the main point to which those topics relate.

_____

_____

Now write that main point as one sentence:

_____

_____

This will be your *working* thesis, the one statement that unifies the entire paper. In many instances, students write a two-part thesis that includes a plan of development or list of subtopics in the thesis. These subtopics will also originate in your note cards. Consider the following examples of such thesis statements.

The very drugs prescribed for depression have serious psychological side effects including depression, increased violent tendencies, and often suicide.

In their attempt to reduce labor costs, American companies that outsource labor support slavelike conditions in sweatshops, cultivate child abuse, and compromise worker safety and health.

While often exaggerated and even humorous, many of Flannery O'Connor's short story characters possess a grotesque quality that is both physical and psychological.

The reason for America's domestic car production slump is threefold: poor workmanship, higher prices due to worker demands, and unregulated influx of foreign cars into the U.S. market.

In the following space, experiment with your thesis. Change the words and sentence structure, but retain your intention. A working thesis can be changed throughout the drafting process; you do not have to decide on a thesis statement until you prepare the final draft of your paper.

Version 1

_____

_____

_____

Version 2

_____

_____

_____

Version 3

_____

_____

_____

More on Writing Thesis Statements

Successful thesis statements often have two parts, the broader identification of the subject and the breakdown into topics of discussion. A semicolon or a colon can be used to separate the two parts.

There are two arguments regarding common use of the "N" word; either it stigmatizes and marginalizes the people it attempts to describe or it neutralizes the word completely, rendering it harmless.

The average person can have an impact on the environment in a variety of ways: using environmentally friendly products, reducing automobile use, eating lighter on the food chain, and recycling.

Mary Shelley's *Frankenstein* is much more than a frightening horror story; it is a warning to humankind against reaching too far beyond one's grasp, a parable about parental responsibilities a creator has to its child, and an example of the destructive consequences of selfishness.

Recently there has been much speculation about the negative effects of antidepressants on the mentally ill; the medical community is researching the reasons for their prescriptions and the side effects of those drugs and issuing warnings about their usage.

In the following space, configure your thesis statement as a two-part sentence.

_____

_____

_____

_____

_____

_____

_____

Sample Thesis Statements

These thesis statements-in-progress demonstrate the range of possibilities within a broader subject, an analysis of Bram Stoker's novel, *Dracula*. Note that some of them still need grammatical and stylistic tweaking (which were evident in multiple drafts of the paper), but the major point of the research has been distilled in one comprehensive sentence.

1. The sexual nature in Dracula includes erotic behavior between characters, women's role during Victorian England, and cross-gendered characteristics. —Saul Garcia

2. In *Dracula*, Bram Stoker incorporates different gothic elements and writing styles. He uses some key gothic literature patterns to create his novel. Bram Stoker creates Count Dracula with Gothic writing elements such as a sense of isolation, characters with monstrous qualities and sexuality in his novel. —Giselle Hereaux

3. Readers can see how Dracula and Jesus had a way of capturing their people with such opposing ways. Dracula is the antithesis, yet is parallel to Jesus because they both emphasize immortality, blood, and moral beliefs. —Ashley Trujillo

4. Stoker reveals the true character of Dracula and emphasizes Gothic fiction through various elements. Two of these distinguishing components include the presence of supernatural beings and monstrosity and patriarchal or tyrannical figures that over-power the women. —Alexandra Vasquez

5. Society's obsession with vampires is associated with the strangeness, universality, gothic nature, and sexuality that were introduced to the myth of the Vampire in Bram Stoker's Dracula. —Alberto Ruiz

6. The popular appeal of horror films is attributed to the adrenaline rush they provide, their ability to induce curiosity and fascination, and the tension of being part of situations vaguely familiar to the individual. —Patricia DeLeon

7. Throughout the novel, Dracula is depicted as the catalyst for women's transition from purity to seductive beings, awakening their concealed desires. —Danays Perera

Analysis: Discussion and Worksheets
Thesis Statements

Name _____   **Date** _____

Thesis Statement Analysis

Following are flawed thesis statements from recent student research papers. Analyze each one and determine how you would refine it. Determine whether the statements are too broad or too narrow and whether they are grammatically correct. Rewrite each one so that it is acceptable.

1. Such as in the Black community where racism has become internalized as an aftermath of the negative influences left behind by slavery which ended almost 400 years ago (Charles 712).

   _____

   _____

   _____

2. The negative effects of steroids in professional sports have affected the morality of many professional sports leagues, its players, and the health of all those teenagers who admire pro athletes.

   _____

   _____

   _____

3. Manufacturers have been producing more fuel efficient car, but the real answer is in alternative fuels.

   _____

   _____

   _____

4. The Muslim, Arabic, Middle Eastern, and Sikh communities have suffered and continue to suffer in the aftermath of the 9/11 tragedy.

   _____

   _____

   _____

5. Our kids are being made more aware but it does not help when they see their idols falling into the trap of steroid use.

_____

_____

_____

6. The mass media's bases are causing Hillary Clinton to receive less coverage than her opponent Barack Obama because of Hillary's overall instability, Obama's rhetorical superiority and race as well as the media's failure in achieving its intended purpose.

_____

_____

_____

7. Video games are changing the world by introducing wide varieties of values that enhances people's minds and promote creative thinking.

_____

_____

_____

8. Who says that video games can only be restricted to entertainment, plenty of video games are being produced for educational purposes.

_____

_____

_____

9. The expansion of electric-engine cars has started to emerge in many important industrial countries in the world. In analyzing them in some significant aspects such as manufacturers, impact economics, population, health and environmental effects, we will determine their usefulness on the planet.

_____

_____

_____

10. There is no excuse for abusing steroids, it does not matter who you are.

_____

_____

_____

Topic Outlines: It's *All* in the Note Cards!

Once your note cards have been completed (about twenty-five to thirty cards), you are ready to begin organizing topics for your paper.

Step 1: Sort and Review Your Note Cards

Review the topic labels on all of your note cards. You might need to make some adjustments. For example, you may have one card that stands out. Can it fit under another topic? Try relabeling it. You might have a very large group of cards under one label. Perhaps you have fifteen of your twenty cards with the same label. Is it too broad? Can you break down the topic and divide the cards into different categories?

Once you have reviewed the content and labels, sort the cards by group. Put all cards with similar labels in separate piles. This is like playing solitaire, putting all the diamonds together, the clubs together, and so on. Stack the cards in small groups.

Step 2: Arrange the Piles in Logical Order

In your paper, which topics should you discuss first? What would make the most sense? Very often, students have topics labeled "history," "origin," or "definition." These topics would be best placed early in the paper. Put all of the piles in sequence.

Step 3: Write a Thesis Statement

Remember that your paper comes directly from your notes. What do your notes say? What is the main point of the research? Formulate a tentative thesis statement that embodies the research focus. Do not worry if it is not perfect; you will have plenty of time to modify it before your final paper.

Step 4: Transfer Topic Labels

Under the thesis, write as many roman numerals as you have topic labels; alongside each, write the topic your paper will cover in the order you have selected. If you have four groups of note cards, you will have four divisions in the topic outline. If you have five groups, then your outline will consist of five divisions. If you have more than seven, you probably need to go back and review your labels again.

Sample Topic Outline

Working thesis: Hybrid cars have many advantages for the consumer and the environment.

   I. History
  II. Economic incentives
 III. Fuel economy
 IV. Environmental impact
  V. Hybrid sales

Topic Outline Form

Name _____   **Date** _____

Fill in the blanks. Write your thesis. Next to each Roman numeral, write your topic.

Thesis:

    I.

    II.

    III.

    IV.

    V.

Congratulations! You have just written your topic outline. Now you have a plan!

Documented Outline Form

Our next step in the research process is to figure out more specifically what to include and where to include it. Again, we allow the note cards to guide us. Using the order of topics in the outline you just completed, you will "plug in" individual note cards in outline subdivisions of A, B, C, and so on. Read each note card carefully and determine what its specific point is. Use a key word to identify the point, and in parentheses, transfer the author and page number of the quotation or paraphrase from the note card to the outline. If you have two different cards on the same topic, use them both. Follow the example of the following documented outline.

Working thesis: Hybrid cars offer many advantages to consumers and the environment.

I. History of hybrid cars

    A. Reasons for development (Smith 76)

    B. First attempts (Aaronson 12)

    C. Current models (Abernathy 6–7)

II. Economic incentives

    A. Government tax breaks (Rogers 18)

    B. Financing incentives (Smith 82)

III. Fuel economy

    A. Gasoline averages (Johnson 137)

    B. Diesel averages (Marshall 3)

    C. Hybrid miles per gallon (Andrews 36) (Smith 56) (Scharf and Ackerman 1)

IV. Environmental impact

    A. Emissions testing (Jonas 104) (Andrews 33)

    B. Reducing greenhouse gases (Abernathy 11) (Ramos 283–4)

V. U.S. hybrid sales

    A. 2000–2005 (Clark 99)

    B. Current sales (Jonas 101) (Smith 79)

    C. Leading manufacturers (Aaronson 16) (Rogers 22)

VI. Conclusion

Preparing a Documented Outline Form Example

Name Lisandra Corvea   **Date** April 23, 2010

Instructions: Convert the information from your topic outline to this form with two additions: (1) expand each topic label into a complete topic sentence; and (2) after each detail, "plug in" the note card you will use by inserting in parentheses the author's last name and page number. You will transfer this information from the note card to this outline and eventually to the final paper. If there is no author or page number, just include the required information as per MLA directions.

Paper title:

Red In the Blood

Thesis statement:

Bram Stoker's Dracula is an exotic novel, for it has several scenes of seduction, sex symbols, and relationships.

I. First supporting point (topic sentence)

The seductive nature within Stoker's characters in the novel is apparent without explicitly including a sexual encounter.

Details (for each detail, include in parentheses the author and page number from the note card alongside the detail; the first detail blank includes the instructions as a reminder)

A. Detail from selected note card (author page number)

Fair vampire seduces Harber (Stoker 39)

B. Dracella seduces Lucy (Frost 2)

C. Animalist seductions (Frost 2)

II. Second supporting point (topic sentence)

The sexual innuendos are further solidified by the use of sexual symbols throughout the story.

Details (for each detail, include in parentheses the author and page number from the note card alongside the detail)

A. Blood = life (Stoker 142)

B. Blood = semen (Frost 2)

C. Blood is an STD (Frost 2)

III. Third supporting point (topic sentence)

The novel has relationships with power exchanges through the swapping of bodily fluids.

Details (for each detail, include in parentheses the author and page number from the note card alongside the detail)

A. Submission (Rosenberg 4)

B. Control (Frost 1)

c. Homoerotic relationship (Stoker 40)

IV. Fourth supporting point (topic sentence)

Details (for each detail, include in parentheses the author and page number from the note card along-side the detail)

A.

B.

C.

V. Fifth supporting point (topic sentence)

Details (for each detail, include in parentheses the author and page number from the note card alongside the detail)

A.

B.

C.

Note: If you have more than six groups, continue with the next Roman numeral.

Preparing a Documented Outline Form

Name _____ **Date** _____

Instructions: Convert the information from your topic outline to this form with two additions: (1) expand each topic label into a complete topic sentence; and (2) after each detail, "plug in" the note card you will use by inserting in parentheses the author's last name and page number. You will transfer this information from the note card to this outline and eventually to the final paper. If there is no author or page number, just include the required information as per MLA directions.

Paper title:

_____

Thesis statement:

_____

_____

   I. First supporting point (topic sentence)

      Details (for each detail, include in parentheses the author and page number from the note card alongside the detail; the first detail blank includes the instructions as a reminder)

      A. Detail from selected note card (author page number)

      B.

C.

II. Second supporting point (topic sentence)

Details (for each detail, include in parentheses the author and page number from the note card alongside the detail)

A.

B.

C.

III. Third supporting point (topic sentence)

Details (for each detail, include in parentheses the author and page number from the note card alongside the detail)

A.

B.

C.

IV. Fourth supporting point (topic sentence or opposing argument)

Details (for each detail, include in parentheses the author and page number from the note card along-side the detail) (Note: If you presented an opposing argument, be sure the details presented support an effective rebuttal.)

A.

B.

C.

V. Fifth supporting point (topic sentence or conclusion/restatement of thesis)

Details (for each detail, include in parentheses the author and page number from the note card alongside the detail)

A.

B.

C.

Note: If you have more than six groups, continue with the next Roman numeral.

After gathering all your material for your research paper and creating your documented outline, you may feel that you do not know where to start with your material or how you are meant to progress with it as you go along in the drafting stages. It helps sometimes to break things down into individual parts, and it is important to just let yourself write. You do not second-guess yourself in the rough draft. You simply *have* to get things down on paper first. After you accomplish that, you can start reviewing the draft itself. Following are various areas that you should review that can help guide you when writing any formal paper, particularly in argumentative style.

Rough Draft Shell

- Write in third person (no *I, me, my, us, we, our,* or *you*).
- Open with an introduction that explains the history or defines the topic that is about to be discussed. (You may use citations that will not be included in the body of the paper. You do not want to repeat citations.)
- Lead to an effective thesis statement by the end of the introduction. (See the sample thesis statements earlier in this chapter.)
- Give each point of development in the thesis statement or topic outline its own section. (It can have multiple paragraphs, but it should be clear by transition when you move on to point II or point III, and so forth.)
- Discuss each point in depth and use the citations from your sources to give support to that reason or point.
- Avoid words like *proves, always, never, everyone,* and so on.
- Use words or phrases like *demonstrates, illustrates, indicates, is evidence of, supports, seems to show,* and so on.
- Avoid putting citations back to back without explanation. Citation after citation without explanation makes for weak arguments.
- *Every* citation should be followed with some kind of explanation, even if it is only a sentence or two. Explain the following:

  What the citation is saying

  Why this information is important

  How this helps argue that point in the paper

- Keep organized according to emphatic order, order of least important to most important.
- For argumentative papers, be sure to include an opposing argument section before you reach your conclusion.

  If you have acquired good sources, they should have already addressed the opposing side. Pick *one* of the opposing points.

  Explain what the opposing point is. (Use sources for support.)

  Explain why this is still not strong enough for anyone to switch to that opposing side.

  Explain what further evidence there is to show that the opposing side is insufficient. (Use sources for support.)

- Conclude with a restatement of the thesis, reemphasizing the main idea and points of development. Close with important thoughts and ideas regarding the topic that will leave your reader thinking about his or her position on the topic. (You may use citations that have not been included in the introduction or body of the paper. Do not repeat any citations.)

Writing the Introduction: Some Pointers

You have been well enough acquainted with your subject to begin to address it generally as if you were talking to the reader. Remember, the purpose of an introductory paragraph is to introduce the thesis statement, and you want to do that with two things in mind: (1) capturing your reader's interest and (2) identifying your subject early on. Your introduction should begin generally and lead to your specific point, stated clearly at the end of the paragraph. Following are some effective openings for beginning your paper. Remember, specific quotes or statistics should be properly cited in order to give credit to the source.

- A startling statement: *The jeans consumers buy at a good price may have cost thousands of underage workers their lives.*

- A surprising statistic: *In America, 75 percent of marriages end in divorce within the first three years.*

- A pertinent quotation: *"I am not a crook."*

- An interesting anecdote: Relate a story that illustrates the major issue of your paper. A recent successful student paper described a grisly gang murder and ended with the revelation that this was typical of a current trend of gang activity—not in the streets but in the U.S. military.

- A thought-provoking question: Draw your reader in with a question that demands attention and compels the reader further.

- A definition: Select and define an inflammatory word related to your subject matter: *Bitch: A lewd or immoral woman,* or *Hoe: An instrument for cultivating, weeding, or loosening the earth.*

- A historical perspective: Offer background information, taking your reader on a historical trip from the past to the present issue to be articulated in the thesis statement.

Whichever method you use, make sure that your introduction is not a skimpy, three-sentence partial paragraph. Your introduction should be carefully developed, gradually and logically leading your reader from the first line to the thesis statement.

Introduction Analysis

Name _____   **Date** _____

Evaluate the following introductory paragraph in the student research paper, "Censorship Beyond the Muggle World." In your evaluation, note what technique the writer uses. Look at the opening line and describe its effectiveness. Note whether the sentences between the opening and the thesis statement flow logically. At the arrival of the thesis statement, note your level of satisfaction.

Gonzalez 1

Dismey Gonzalez

Professor Shaw

English 1102

25 April 2008

Censorship Beyond the Muggle World

For centuries, free speech and writing have gone hand in hand with censorship. Authorities have always sought to discourage certain ideas that may be offensive or disruptive, and have done so by censoring means of communication that would otherwise allow freedom of expression. Censorship has many faces: it ranges from prohibiting certain ideas to forbidding specific words to be said or written. The assimilation of Native American children into Christian schools is a perfect example of how the United States enacted this form of political control. Said children were disallowed from speaking their native tongue to "cleanse" them of their Native American taint. Harsh punishments followed those who violated the rules, including being force-fed bars of soap. Today, censorship has become a popular tool through which political and religious groups (among others) have sought to silence opposition or remove threats to their popularity. It is not limited to pulling books from library shelves; it can be seen every day in movies, TV shows, periodicals and other forms of communication. As much as it has been used in the past, censorship is presently applied in much the same manner, as may be witnessed with the phenomenon around a boy wizard whose toughest battle has been proved to be against freedom of expression.

Sample Argumentative Paper Layout in MLA Format

LN (Last Name) Page	**LN Page**	**LN Page**
	Reason A	Reason B
Your Name		
Prof Name		
Class		
Date		
Title		
Introduction		
Thesis statement: Topic + Stand + A + B + C		

LN Page	**LN Page**	**LN Page**
Reason C	Opposing Argument with Rebuttal	Works Cited
	Restatement of Thesis with Conclusion	

Sample Student Papers with Commentary

Sometimes it can help to see specific examples of papers from students that have, in fact, already followed this process and have completed a research paper. We have provided sample student papers that illustrate some of the ideas we have discussed.

When reviewing the student papers, pay special attention to the following:

1. Introduction:

    Does it open with an attention-getting statement?

    Is it developed enough to gracefully lead to the thesis?

    Does the thesis logically follow its preceding sentence?

2. Body sections:

    Does each section begin with a topic sentence?

    Does the supporting evidence relate directly to that sentence?

    Does the writer use transitions within the section?

    Does the section contain sufficient support?

3. Documentation:

    Is all the researched information clearly identified?

    Does the writer use enough signal phrases to introduce that material?

    Do parenthetical citations appear at the end of the borrowed words?

    Are longer quotations properly indented and punctuated?

    Does the Works Cited page include every source that appeared in the paper?

    Are there any floating quotations?

    Are the signal phrases varied so the paper doesn't feel repetitive?

4. Conclusion:

    Does the conclusion balance the introduction in terms of length and development?

    Does it neatly "wrap the package"?

    Does it restate without repeating?

    Does it leave the reader thinking?

After reviewing these questions for the following sample papers, you want to be able to answer these questions for your own written work as well. Seeing a model is a beginning. The important thing to remember is that after following the process completely, which includes revising multiple drafts as these students did, you should be able to answer "yes" to all of these questions for your own research paper also.

Susan Valdes

Prof. Olaguibel-Lundahl

ENC1102

10 December 2009

Embryonic Stem Cell Research

Bellomo concurs, ". . . the possibilities just seem too great to ignore" (148). From this quote, one can see that embryonic stem cell (ES) research has opened a great window of hope for many people suffering from illnesses because of all the potential benefits they hold. ES research may be the answer people have been waiting for. How are these cells attained? The first concept to understand is the formation of a zygote. According to Balint, "When a spermatozoon enters an ovum and its DNA is introduced into the nucleus of the ovum, this DNA pairs up with the corresponding DNA already in the nucleus of the ovum, reconstituting its total genetic material in forty-six chromo-somes" (729-730). It is important to understand the formation of a zygote because embryonic stem cells are ultimately derived from mul-tiple divisions of a zygote. Balint further explains that, ". . . the zygote starts to divide if conditions are favorable; first to form a blastomere of eight, then sixteen cells, and ultimately to form around day five a blas-tocyst. The blastocyst consists of 120 to 150 cells, some of which are the stem cells that can develop into all forms of normal human tissue" (729-730). This is also essential to understand because in order to take ES cells for research, this process would have to take place first. These cells have great potential because they can become anything the human body may need.

> Very nice job providing a working definition and background for the topic.

ES research would change the lives of millions of ill people. It is a topic that has much debate on moral, ethical and legal stands. Many of its opponents argue that it is unethical to do ES research because the embryonic mass of cells is an individual with human rights. However, embryonic stem cell research should be permitted because they hold potential cures for many diseases, they can be very useful for organ transplantation and because there is a surplus of discarded embryos from in vitro fertilization (IVF) that can be used for research.

> Explain a bit more here why it is so debatable.

> Very clear thesis statement. You show well what stand you will be arguing and what reasons you will be develop-ing for that stand.

Embryonic stem cell research should be permitted because it holds potential cures for many diseases. Today, many Americans are waiting and hoping for a cure for their illnesses. According to Perry, people who may benefit from ES cells are the 58 million with cardiovascular

> Clear topic sentence to start this section.

Valdez 2

> Good explanation of significance of information.

> Again, good analysis of information.

> Okay transition to next section.

> Good.

> Good.

disease, 30 million with autoimmune disease, 16 million with diabetes, 10 million with osteoporosis, 8.2 million with cancer, 4 million with Alzheimer's disease, 1.5 million with Parkinson's, 0.3 with people who have been severely burnt, 0.25 with spinal cord injuries, and 150,000 of babies with birth defects per year. That is a total of 128.4 million people (170). These numbers demonstrate that ES research is greatly needed. What a great accomplishment it would be to be able to heal such an incredible number of people. It would be an immense number of lives that would be changed. According to McGee and Caplan, ". . . more humans die every year from cancer than were killed in both Kosovo and Vietnam conflicts. Stem cell research is a pursuit of known and important moral goods" (154). It is sad that so many people are dying from illnesses when there is a potential answer to their problems at the country's fingertips. Why should a cure be denied to these people? Why should the United States watch its citizens and their families suffer daily from the hassles and the burdens of being ill? It is not just to deny anyone a right to be healthy when a cure is waiting to be put into action. Even though scientists believe ES cells can cure many diseases, research is currently not allowed on humans (Bellomo 152). This shows that the United States is not doing everything in its power to heal citizens. The United States would not just be allowing research to be done, they would be freeing millions of Americans from their illnesses and they would be giving the right to live a healthy life.

Another reason to allow embryonic stem cell research is because it can be used for organ transplantations. According to Bellomo, "Embryonic stem cells, which are extracted from the fifth day of the embryo's blastocyst formation, have such a high degree of developmental plasticity that they are capable of becoming any type of cell in the body" (146). This shows that with these cells, scientists would be able to grow any body organ that may be needed. Wright reports, "Embryonic stem cells could be grown as universal graft tissue for blood, bone marrow, lung, liver, kidney, tendons, ligaments, muscle, skin, hair, teeth, the retina and the lens of the eye" (6). This illustrates the many benefits of ES research. All of these parts are important and have their significant function in the human body. Today, what would happen if a person needed a kidney transplant and there was no suitable donor? The patient would most likely die because of the shortage of kidney donations. People who have been physically hurt or who have diseases where new tissue is needed, won't have to stress over finding a matching donor (Wright 2). From this, one can imply that mortality rates would decrease for those in need of transplants. Wright explains, "Another way to prevent graft rejection is to substitute the embryonic stem-cell nucleus for a nucleus from a healthy cell of the patient. The resulting graft tissue would genetically match the patient's tissue" (6). This makes it clear that by using embryonic stem cells, if someone is in need of a kidney they would not have to wait to find a suitable donor. Organs would be accessible for anyone who needs one.

According to the Uniform Anatomical Gift Act, "In the case of children, parents are the primary decision makers on the issue of organ donation" (qtd. in Dolin 1238). Therefore, a mother should be allowed to make a decision to donate her embryos if she so chooses because she is its decision maker. These embryos are potential organs, and if the mother does not want it or if it is going to be tossed out from IVF, it should be used for research. This will at least give the embryo use by providing an organ to someone who is in much need of one. Dolin observes that if science never explored and studied new ideas, there would not be any treatments because in order to have advancement there must be exploration (1240). This is true for any new discovery. If no one attempts to find an answer, chances are they will never find one. Until the United States begins to conduct research with embryonic stem cells, the country will not be able to benefit from all the potential these cells have to help society.

Finally, embryonic stem cell research should be allowed because there are many embryos that are not used after IVF that have more potential than to simply be discarded. This complex procedure is done mostly with families that need assistance with fertility. With IVF, eight to fifteen oocytes are removed from the woman's ovaries (Dolin 1212). This demonstrates that IVF is a complex process which is done for people who are serious about growing a family. Dolin goes on to explain that, "Between forty percent and seventy percent of the retrieved oocytes undergo fertilization successfully. Eggs that are successfully fertilized are then implanted, stored, or discarded" (1212-1213). From this, one can see that if embryos were used for research rather than be discarded, they would have the potential to save lives. According to Dolin, "There are currently roughly 400,000 frozen

Valdez 3

You do a very nice job of analyzing each piece of text that you bring in. Well done.

Good return to stand here.

You stay nicely consistent with thesis order.

Valdez 4

embryos being kept in a variety of labs across the United States. At the same time, Nightlight Christian Adoptions-the pre-eminent embryo adoption network- has completed only 2410 embryo adoptions in 10 years" (1251). From this quote, one can see that adoption of embryos is not a solution to the surplus of embryos that exist. There are not enough people to adopt the large number of unused embryos. Therefore, the next best thing that can be done with these embryos is to use them for research. They have two choices, to be discarded and serve no purpose whatsoever or they can be used for research where they have the potential to save another life and contribute to mankind.

You are making good assertions based on the information you're using.

Also, when embryos are created for the purpose of IVF, the couple realizes that there is a good chance that many of these embryos will not be used. As parents, they have authority to decide what should happen to these embryos. Dolin points out, "State courts have also accepted the proposition that when a patient is incompetent, a surrogate, who is more often than not a close family member, can make a decision on the patient's behalf" (1228). In this case, where the embryo is the patient, it cannot make its own decisions. Dolin argues that embryos that are kept in storage are similar to kids that are being kept alive with life support and that the surrogate can choose what to do with them (1231). This demonstrates that the life of the embryo is considered just as seriously as the life of a child. Under difficult situations like such, parents are put into a hard spot. No parent wants their child to die. They do want to do what they feel is best for their child in a difficult situation. The same goes for these surplus embryos. The parents care about this potential being, but they also need to weigh their options and make the most suitable decision. If an embryo is not to be supplied with life, the best choice would be to give this embryo some sort of purpose.

Good.

McCartney reports, "It seems to me that the derivation of embryonic stem cells from embryos that have been frozen in the process of in vitro fertilization, in some instances, be seen as the lesser of two evils and the approach that respects life more genuinely than thawing and destroying, and this should be considered ethical" (615). This shows that the author is in agreement that this process is not unethical as many perceive it to be. According to Wright, "Human embryonic stem cells that have already been collected may be a sufficient source of cells for future replacement tissue so that no new embryos are required" (2). This supports that ES research will not necessarily need to destroy millions of embryos because there are already many available. This overload of embryos can save such a large number of people that it would be a waste to just toss them to destruction without giving them a chance to be something important in this world.

Opponents would argue that it would be unethical to take stem cells from embryos because the embryo is an individual with human rights. However, one can see that these cell masses lack many human characteristics and are not yet to be labeled as an individual. According to McCartney, "Up until the formation of the primitive streak, which will develop into the spinal cord, and cell differentiation, which occurs about fourteen days after fertilization, the developing embryo can cleave naturally or artificially, resulting in the production of identical siblings" (601-602). From this quote one can see that if twinning is still possible, this embryo should not be labeled as an individual. It can divide and be made into two separate individuals, meaning that it is not yet its own self. McGee and Caplan explain, "The human embryo from which stem cells are to be taken is an undifferentiated embryo. It contains mitochondria, cytoplasm, and the DNA of mother and father within an egg wall. None of the identity of that embryo is wrapped up in its memory of its origins: it has no brain cells to think no muscle cells to exercise, no habits" (154). The embryo doesn't even know it is alive. It has no capacity to think or recognize that it is an embryo. All it is at that point is a mass of cells. An individual is someone who can think for itself, has its own ideas and its own mind. Infants, who cannot think rationally, can be considered individuals because they interpret stimuli in their own way. Their minds can choose to move in the ways they want. They feel pain, hunger, fear and much more emotions. A mass of cells can do none of these things.

Bush states he has been told that, "A five day cluster of cells is not an embryo, not yet an individual, but a pre-embryo . . . it has potential for life, but it is not a life because it cannot develop on its own" (11). Here, one can see that scientists who have researched this matter to inform the former president agree that an individual is one who can develop and respond on its own to its environment. Balint states, ". . . scholars and others contend that the embryo to be destroyed in the process of recovering their stem cells have not, at the blastocyst stage, attained human personhood or individuality; and, further, that human

Valdez 5

Excellent support in this third reason. You build nicely from your first to last reason in emphatic order.

Good opposing idea, but explain their reasoning a little; demonstrate that you understand fully why they say this.

Valdez 6

Very nice support for rebuttal. You address the opposing side's concern very well with text to back up your assertions.

Clear restatement of thesis.

embryos at this stage do not have rights—a position supported by the courts" (738-739). This would mean that the embryo has no personality. It has no thoughts, no feelings or memories. This embryo should not be considered a human individual and therefore is not yet granted its human rights.

To conclude, embryonic stem cell research should be permitted because they hold potential cures for many diseases, they can be very useful for organ transplantation and because there is a surplus of discarded embryos from in vitro fertilization that can be used for research. According to Wright, "Human embryonic stem cells may also provide a means to study the progression of human disease and find effective, permanent treatments. Human embryonic stem cells will also be useful for studying the normal differentiation process to enhance our understanding of human development" (6). One can see that medical advancements will skyrocket and make this generation known for all the lives that would be drastically changed. Medical professionals will have a greater understanding of the human body and its functions. They will also feel at ease knowing that there is hope for all the sick people in the United States and that they will actually be able to do something to help their patients. Goodell states, "Embryonic stem cells have great potential. The last thing we should do is restrict research" (qtd. in Vogel 57). This demonstrates that this is an important issue that should be supported. If society allowed embryonic stem cell research, they would open a door to a better future for many people. Many will benefit because most people will face some sort of illness in their life or have a family member who will be ill at some point. Society knows what it is like to feel fear and anger towards illnesses that they have no control over. How would the society feel if they understood that the government is keeping potential cures from them and restricting them from the healthier life they could live? Doing so would be unjust to the American society. Balint believes, ". . . there is a duty to find remedies for disease, that the future good will in fact outweighs the harm of embryo destruction, and that federal funding of such research is the only way to ensure equity in the distribution of benefits to all members of society" (738). One can see that it is in fact a duty for medical professionals to do anything in their power to help the society be in as healthy of a state as can be. Society should not be restricted of potential cures.

Excellent closing quote and final thoughts. It leaves the reader thinking about the topic.

Works Cited

Balint, John A. "Ethical Issues in Stem Cell Research." *Albany Law Review* 65.3 (2002): 729-43. *Academic Onefile.* Gale. Miami Dade College. 11 Nov. 2009 <http://find.galegroup.com>.

Dolin, Gregory. "A Defense of Embryonic Stem Cell Research." *Indiana Law Journal* 84.4 (2009): 1203-57. *Academic Search Complete.* EBSCO. Miami Dade College. 18 Nov. 2009 <http://web.ebsco-host.com>.

McCartney, James J. "Embryonic Stem Cell Research and Respect for Human Life: Philosophical and Legal Reflections." *Albany Law Review* 65.3 (2002): 597-625. *Academic Onefile.* Gale. Miami Dade College. 11 Nov. 2009 <http://find.galegroup.com>.

Michael, Bellomo. *The Stem Cell Divide.* New York: Amacom, 2006.

Perry, Daniel, et al. *The Stem Cell Controversy.* Ed. Michael Ruse and Christopher A. Pynes. Amherst: Prometheus Books, 2003.

Wright, Shirley J. "Human Embryonic Stem-Cell Research: Science and Ethics." *American Scientist* 87.4 (1999): 352-61. *General Science Full Text.* Wilson. Miami Dade College. 18 Nov. 2009 <http://vnweb.hwwilsonweb.com>.

Good overall MLA in your in-text citations and works cited entries; remember that MLA has modified some of its works cited entries for database articles. Be sure to review the new guidelines for future papers.

Yesenia Hernandez

Professor J. Lundahl

ENC 1102

30 November 2009

The Patriot Act

On September 11, 2001, a terrorist group called al-Qaeda attacked the Twin Towers of the World Trade Center and the Pentagon; the plan was also to attack the White House, but fortunately that part of the plan was unsuccessful. About three thousand people were killed and several thousand were injured (Brasch 2). The United States legislative and executive system retaliated by passing the Uniting and Strengthening America by Providing Appropriate Tools Required to Intercept and Obstruct Terrorism Act of 2001, also known as the USA Patriot Act or the Patriot Act to assist in the fight against terrorism and protect the United States from the same degrading fate as what had occurred on that day (Brasch 4). The USA Patriot Act was enacted unanimously. However, there have been claims that the Patriot Act contradicts existing laws in the United States Constitution and that the government has abused its liberal powers granted by it. The USA Patriot Act should not be renewed because it permits the government to operate in excessive secrecy, it gives the government excess power, and it violates the United States Constitution.

The Patriot Act should not be reestablished into law because it gives the state the power to rein in excess secrecy. Parts of the Act have been written to favor the government. The Freedom of Information Act (FOIA) is a law that stipulates public access to records pertaining to the U.S. government; however, there are some statutes that emphasize confidentiality as well. Generally, the Freedom of Information Act (FOIA) was once in favor of letting the public know of information, but since 9/11, the new policy aims to emphasize disclosure on a need to know basis (Wong 174). This suggests that the government is so secretive that it keeps information from the media and that information therefore remains unchecked. The media informs the public of an event/incident and the public pressures its lawmakers into correcting the incident/event and/or trying to prevent it from happening again. Through this act, the government has consented to secret searches and surveillance and indefinite detentions without letting the public know. Secrecy has a way of leading to abused unchecked power. The

Good brief background and definition. Perhaps expand just a bit more on the process of it passing so that the debate is fully understood.

Expand on this just a bit more as well.

Good, clear thesis statement. Your stand is solid with good reasons for development.

Clear topic sentence here.

You do a good job here of explaining why the information from text is significant.

Act has granted the government the power "to monitor, investigate, detain, and deport Muslims legally in the name of security, without rudimentary due process of the law and in gross violation of their rights" (Wong 165). As a result of this they have been singled out and mistreated severely. The media would be useful in this situation because the media indirectly checks the government; when the media informs the public they stir their lawmakers into preventing the event/incident from happening again if it is illegal or problem enhancing. Unfortunately, "for security purposes, for the state to operate freely without having to justify itself to the public in order to serve its purpose secrecy from media services must be obtained" (Michaels 258). If the media does not bring out actions of the government then, they can act freely without having to worry about justifying themselves in the eyes of the public; that worrying usually keeps the government in check from abusing power and violating its very own law. Too much secrecy is not good for the overall health of the nation and its infrastructure. The Act should not be renewed because it promotes secrecy which harms everything that democracy stands for.

Too much secrecy has a tendency of leading to too much power and that leads to the manipulation of power. The USA Patriot Act should not be renewed because it grants federal/state governments too much power. An example of this is National Security Letters. National Security Letters (NSLs) are subpoenas used by the FBI and other U.S. government agencies that require no probable cause or any oversight by the judicial system and when an individual/entity is served with them they cannot say that they received it (Weigel 73). The Patriot Act enables the government to operate on many instances on an unchecked power basis and situations like the misuse of NSLs take place (Gorham-Oscilowski and Jaeger 629). As a result, the Department of Justice revealed in its DoJ Report that there were "an array of different circumstances under which NSLs were improperly or illegally issued and used, including requests for improper information, lack of necessary approvals, and unauthorized collection of information" (Gorham-Oscilowski and Jaeger 629). When little power is given especially unchecked, it can accumulate especially when there is secrecy preventing the public from knowing; little power goes unnoticed and then all of a sudden it accumulates and it is uncontrollable. History is evidence that too much power leads to destructive circumstances

Interesting assertion.

Good return to your stand here.

Good topic sentence to indicate beginning of new section.

This shows? Explain before going on to next citation; you don't want citations back to back without expanding a bit in your own words.

Good!

Hernandez 3

Interesting parallel here.

Good use of text to return to stand.

Good.

Good use of questioning to make your point here.

(Hurwitz 20). For instance, in Germany, Hitler, the Reich President, would have everyone label their material possessions and this was the start of control. Little by little he was able to control the media. Hitler would use the media to his favor and his authority would be unchecked and remain that way. Then he slowly began to classify Germans according to race, religion, etc., and he acquired so much power from the little that he started with that a World War was born and a catastrophe was instituted. People were murdered, mass executions took place and all of this was because of the start of a little bit of power given to a governing body and an unchecked one at that. Calamity and foul behavior is the direct/indirect result of a sovereign body in possession of extreme supremacy. The Patriot Act could inspire unwanted harmful events and incidents because it allows the government to reign in a dangerous amount of unsafe power. The government should not have too little or too much power but a balance so that no right is violated as the following quote suggests: "We must be on constant guard against an excessive use of any power, military, or otherwise, that results in the needless destruction of our rights and liberties. There must be a careful balancing of interest" (qtd. in Brasch 50).

Finally, the Patriot Act should not be renewed because it violates the foundation of this country: The United States Constitution—the supreme law of the land. A pen/trap is a form of electronic surveillance used by government agencies in the United States. One of the Sections of the Patriot Act allows any obtained pen/trap order valid throughout the entire country (Henderson 202). So, any specific pen-trap order stating a particular location is valid anywhere in the United States and this conflicts with the Fourth Amendment of the Constitution, specifically one of the amendments in the Bill of Rights, because one of the requirements for a warrant is that the location/place that will be searched is named specifically (Henderson 202). In the fourth amendment of the Constitution, it states that a valid warrant must specify location. If the Act encourages violation of the Constitution and/or circumvents the law that is necessary to protect individuals from the government, what will protect them when the law necessary to protect them is deemed useless in that situation? This is the law stipulated in the Constitution; it is written in blood. And yet, the governing system has found a way to bypass its very own creation and one of the oldest foundations of this country. The Patriot Act is further encouraging the government to protest democracy because democracy in this nation is the Bill of Rights that the government is violating in order to fight terrorism. When people easily acquiesce on such important matters it can become a habit and the very own tool necessary to protect them is deemed useless in the matter when they need it the most.

> The fact that as the year 2002 began, some 600 to 700 noncitizens remained incarcerated with no assurances of legal representation or even a guarantee that either charges would be filed against them or that they would be released within a specific timeframe, should serve as a red flag that we are losing the traditional American virtue of political and legal restraint (Davis 8).

Good setting off of long quote according to MLA.

Immigrants and even citizens have been abused by the United States government and the Constitution which is their protector is not valid in any of these situations in the eyes of the federal government. People have been arrested and treated cruelly because they voice their dissent about the Patriot Act; this violates the First Amendment of the Constitution (Davis 6). The Act continuously violates the Constitution. The fact that the government perceives the situation to how they deemed correct [having the immigrants incarcerated with not being able to see their lawyer or being guaranteed that they will be charged with a crime and having people treated cruelly] supports the idea that the government is given too much power by the Patriot Act and that they violate that power and laws associated with it. The Global Policy form stipulates that the Patriot Act violates the following Amendments of the United States Constitution: First, Fourth, Fifth, Sixth, Seventh, Eighth, and Thirteenth; it gives authorities the power to circumvent and/or completely disregard these rights which most are in the Bill of Rights (Barr 34-35). The Bill of Rights is what the founding fathers sweated for and battled for because the government at that time was controlling them and imposing cruelty among them. The Bill of Rights makes the Constitution unique from the laws of other countries because its aim is to protect its individual citizens from maltreatment. The Patriot Act directly/ indirectly prevents protection from the government and this could result in the persecution of innocents and it could be the cause of a great disaster. It upheavals what the United States is—a democracy.

Good point.

Hernandez 5

There is no judicial overview implemented when it is time to review government actions and its powers to enforce it rulings (Michaels 235). This supports the idea that the government is violating its own law because the system is set up to check itself by one branch checking up on the other [in this instance, the judicial branch of the government checking the legislative branch part in charge of government agencies in terms of monitoring agency decisions, actions, and operations]. The government is encouraged by the Patriot Act to move the nation backwards not forward because it is violating its own mandate so, what will keep it from further self-destruction? It is causing its own annihilation because what it stands for, its values and laws that have kept it from entering a ruin are being desecrated and those laws are meant to keep the entire governing system in equilibrium. However, with its disequilibrium a catastrophe internally and externally awaits. The USA Patriot Act should not be renewed because it allows the violating of the Constitution which weakens the nation into a peril state that can result in a catastrophe.

The opposing side agrees that Patriot Act should be renewed because it gives the U.S. government more powers necessary to combat terrorism. "Terrorism requires the creation of new laws to protect domestic land from vile acts even if those laws be more intrusive than others" (Koch 25). The opposing side supports the Patriot Act because they feel that it ensures the protection of its citizens against terrorists and that it catches terrorists efficiently and effectively. However, according to former House Representative Bob Barr, the measures to resist and combat terrorism already exist (34-35). The information that could have alerted government officials that a plot like 9/11 was going to take place was already within their possession, but government intelligence failed to detect it (Barr 34). More power and money does not ensure a successful intervention of such vile acts. On the contraire, more power leads to manipulation, misuse and abuse. Cicero concurred that "laws are silent when arms are raised" (qtd. in Brasch 4). This supports the idea that "in time of war, the laws fall silent" (qtd. in Brasch 4). There is too much emphasis on giving the government too much power, letting it secretly maneuver to what its own perception deems right, and allowing it to circumvent laws when it feels necessary to do so.

> Very interesting third reason and you develop your reasons well in emphatic order.

> Good explanation of opposing side reasoning.

> Good answer to opposing side. Elaborate more what exactly is in place.

> Good.

The USA Patriot Act should not be reenacted because it allows the government to work in excessive secrecy, it gives the government excessive power, and it violates existing laws in the United States Constitution. America's spirit is based on freedom and individual rights written in the United States Constitution (Davis 14).

Good restatement of thesis.

Add a bit more in your own words before going on to next citation.

Americans crave freedom—unabashed, unmolested, unfettered freedom. And, that freedom ultimately must exist for all who call themselves American or the grand experiment fails. We must think along and hard about the threats facing us and the consequences of proposed security measure before we acquiesce to laws and customs that violate the spirit of freedom that is the nation's bedrock principle (Davis 14).

The Constitution is a belief system and if that system is violated then chaos erupts because people do not like their belief system, the foundation of how they live their lives, to be disrupted and torn down. It is the basis of the country and other existing laws. The system will collapse with its violation. "Rev. Martin Luther King, Jr., said it best—a nation that continually devotes its resources to programs of war rather than to programs of national uplift is approaching spiritual death" (Michaels 427). Ever since that destructive day [9/11], everything has been toward assuring security and safety of the domestic land and its inhabitants by giving up power and unfortunately the nation's spirit is slowly withering. Granting government officials more power, secrecy, and the authority to circumvent laws does not ensure safety it actually demotes it because people begin to fear for their safety against their very own government.

Nicely strong closing thoughts.

Hernandez 7

Works Cited

Barr, Bob. "The United States Does Not Need the Patriot Act to Fight Terror." *The Patriot Act*. Ed. Lauri S. Friedman. Farmington Hills: Greenhaven Press, 2009. 32-37.

Brasch, Walter M. *America's Unpatriotic Acts: The Federal Government's Violation of Constitutional and Civil Rights*. New York City: Peter Lang Publishing, 2005.

Davis, Derek H. "The Dark Side to a Just War: The USA Patriot Act and Counterterrorism's Potential Threat to Religious Freedom." *Journal of Church and State 44.1 (2002): 5-17. Legal Periodicals & Books*. Wilson. Miami Dade College North. 18 Nov. 2009 <http://vnweb.hwwilsonweb.com>.

Gorham-Oscilowski, Ursula, and Paul T. Jaeger. "National Security Letters, the USA PATRIOT ACT, and the Constitution: The Tensions between National Security and Civil Rights." *Government Information Quarterly* 25 (2008): 625-44. *OmniFile Full Text Mega Edition*. Wilson. Miami Dade College North. 16 Nov. 2009 <http://vnweb.hwwilsonweb.com>.

Henderson, Nathan C. "The Patriot Act's Impact on the Government's Ability to Conduct Electronic Surveillance of Ongoing Domestic Communications." *Duke Law Journal* 52 (2002): 179-209. *Academic OneFile*. Gale. Miami Dade College North. 16 Nov. 2009 <http://find.galegroup.com>.

Hurwitz, Julie. "The Patriot Act Is Not a Good Antiterrorism Tool." *The Patriot Act*. Ed. Lauri S. Friedman. Farmington Hills: Greenhaven Press, 2009. 18-24.

Koch, Edward I. "The United States Needs the Patriot Act to Fight Terror." *The Patriot Act*. Ed. Lauri S. Friedman. Farmington Hills: Greenhaven Press, 2009. 25-31.

Michaels, C. William. *No Greater Threat: America After September 11 and the Rise of a National Security State*. 2nd ed. Rev. ed. New York City: Algora Publishing, 2005.

Weigel, David. "The Powers Granted in the Patriot Act Have Been Abused." *The Patriot Act*. Ed. Lauri S. Friedman. Farmington Hills: Greenhaven Press, 2009. 68-74.

Wong, Kam C. "The USA Patriot Act: A Policy of Alienation." *Michigan Journal of Race & Law* 12.1 (2006): 161-202. *Legal Periodicals & Books*. Wilson. Miami Dade College North. 18 Nov. 2009 <http://vnweb.hwwilsonweb.com>.

> Good overall MLA, in-text and in the works cited. Remember that MLA has now modified some guidelines, especially for database articles. Keep that in mind when you construct your papers in the future.

Dismey Gonzalez

Professor Shaw

English 1102

25 April 2008

Censorship Beyond the Muggle World

For centuries, free speech and writing have gone hand in hand with censorship. Authorities have always sought to discourage certain ideas that may be offensive or disruptive, and have done so by censoring means of communication that would otherwise allow freedom of expression. Censorship has many faces: it ranges from prohibiting certain ideas to forbidding specific words to be said or written. The assimilation of Native American children into Christian schools is a perfect example of how the United States enacted this form of political control. Said children were disallowed from speaking their native tongue to "cleanse" them of their Native American taint. Harsh punishments followed those who violated the rules, including being force-fed bars of soap. Today, censorship has become a popular tool through which political and religious groups (among others) have sought to silence opposition or remove threats to their popularity. It is not limited to pulling books from library shelves; it can be seen every day in movies, TV shows, periodicals and other forms of communication. As much as it has been used in the past, censorship is presently applied in much the same manner, as may be witnessed with the phenomenon around a boy wizard whose toughest battle has been proved to be against freedom of expression.

The first law of censorship dates back to 300 AD in China (Newth). Authorities felt that part of a good government's responsibility was to make sure that the citizens were righteous individuals, and censoring their ideas was a way to shape them into whom they ought to be. Back then, punishment for those who dishonored "the moral and political code" was severe (Newth). Such is the case of Socrates, who in 399 BC was forced to drink poison for his "corruption of youth and his acknowledgement of unorthodox divinities" (Newth). After the printing press was invented, King Henry VIII of England required that all materials to be printed be approved by the Church of England first, thus censoring all those whom the Church was not in accord with. In America, the first act of censorship happened in the form of the burning of a book, in 1650 in Massachusetts. A man called William Pynchon wrote a booklet about religion that was later confiscated and burned by Puritan authorities (Mullally).

While the banning of books is a practice as old as time, it is by no means an abolished one. According to the American Library Association, classics like Mark Twain's The Adventures of Huckleberry Fin and Of Mice and Men by John Steinbeck ranked among the 10 most often disputed books in 1990-2000 due to the violence and harsh language within them. The number one spot as the most challenged book series goes to one of the most popular and best selling books of the century: The Harry Potter series (Kennedy). Written by British author J. K. Rowling, the books follow the story of a neglected boy who, on his 11th birthday learns that he is a wizard and goes off to a boarding school to learn magic. Trouble and adventure ensues when an evil wizard who terrorized the magic community years prior and whom Harry unknowingly defeated as a baby, comes back to take revenge on the boy. The books have been the target of several attacks by many who claim that they promote witchcraft and contain references to Satanism and the occult as good practices.

There have been numerous challenges against Harry Potter, many of them stemming from a religious point of view. "Christians see it as a battle between good and evil for the souls of Britain's children" says Neil Mackay in his article "Witches' War with Church for Kids' Souls." They see the books as a threat against Christianity because they see them as a window to what is becoming the latest "trend" in religion: Paganism. "Christians don't like it" adds Mackay, "particularly as their congregations are

Gonzalez 3

plummeting." With claims that books such as the Harry Potter series encourages

teenagers to explore other religions that "can seriously damage your spiritual and

psychological health", the Christian Church has taken action against them and tried to

prohibit them in several schools all over Britain. John Buckeridge, editor of the

Christian magazine "Youthwork" opines about Rowling's series that "on one level it's just

a good read, but on another level it's softening the path for Paganism to become part of

mainstream society."

In reality, the church is fighting a battle against itself. Those who have read the

books enjoy them for what they are: the adventures of a boy who lives in a magical world

where snakes talk and entertainment comes in the form of flying brooms and moving

chess. Most readers wouldn't have noted the alleged references to an occult religion had

it not been pointed out to them. Rowling's books don't push readers towards a specific

religion. Actually, they don't invite them to explore any religion at all. If people have

become curious about other religions after reading the Potter series, they have probably

done so because of the all the commotion around it from religious authorities in the first

place. They are interested in seeing what all the fuzz is about and if the books really have

a relation to these religions. The truth is that these Christians are not accepting of any

religion besides their own. Had the Potter books talked about Christianity in a good

light, the story would be completely different. The books would be highly accepted and

even recommended among the Christian community.

While usually the biggest one, religion is not the only reason to ban books.

Different cultural and social customs, sexual references and age-appropriate content

(especially on children's books) are often at the center of book censorship. In the article

"Harry Potter the New Gay Icon?" writer Liam McDougall compares similarities of Harry

Potter's story to that of a "traditional coming-out story." Parallels such as Harry being

seen as "abnormal" in the eyes of his relatives just as much as a gay person may be seen in front of heterosexuals, and the censorship over certain words (Harry's aunt and uncle forbid him to bring up "the M word" – magic) "very much lends itself to actual society, where there is still a strong feeling that the G-word or the H-word should not be mentioned" says Michael Bronski, author of "Culture Clash: The Making of Gay Sensibility" (McDougall 1). While Bronski enforces that he does not believe the Potter books were written specifically in a gay reading subtext, he does think that Rowling appears to "play more openly" with it. It is no surprise then, that in a recent interview with the Potter writer where she admitted that she always saw character Dumbledore, Headmaster of Hogwarts (the school where Harry and his friends learn magic) as gay, the homosexual community saw a light of acceptance in her books, since Dumbledore is one of the most powerful characters in the series. When asked why she hadn't openly portrayed Dumbledore as gay in the books, she answered that "her revelation about Dumbledore would give them [Christian groups] one more reason" to find the books objectionable ("JK Rowling outs Dumbledore").

Amusingly enough, most people who present challenges against these books and argue that they are not suitable to keep in school libraries, have never actually read them. Such is the case of Laura Mallory, a Georgia mother who has appeared in court several times in the last few years in attempts to remove the Harry Potter books from school shelves. She asserts that the books "indoctrinate children as Wiccans, or practitioners of religious witchcraft" and, although a gunshot is never even mentioned throughout the series, that they "help foster the kind of culture where school shootings happen" ("Ban Harry Potter 1"). Despite her many efforts and appeals, the Potter books yet remain to be removed from school libraries.

One of the leading arguments against book censorship is that it goes against our Nation's First Amendment, which states that "Congress shall make no law respecting an establishment of religion, or prohibiting the free exercise thereof; or abridging the

Gonzalez 5

freedom of speech, or of the press; or the right of the people peaceably to assemble, and

to petition the government for a redress of grievances" (U.S. Constitution). Perhaps the

most important case in reference to school libraries banning books and the First

Amendment is the Pico case in 1981, in which high school students led by Steven Pico

argued with school boards about "denial of their First Amendment rights" at the U.S.

District Court (Mullally). The case escalated all the way to the U.S. Supreme Court, who

voted 5-4 for the students and declared, "Local school boards may not remove books

from school library shelves simply because they dislike the ideas contained in those

books..." (Mullally).   *Consecutive citations*

Several organizations and events have been formed to fight book banning and

suppression. KidSPEAK (formerly known as Muggles for Harry Potter) is a campaign

born from the attempts to ban the Harry Potter books, which gives children a voice to

defend their right to read books without censorship. The American Library Association

celebrates Banned Books Week every year under the slogan "Free People Read Freely" in

hopes to make readers aware of their rights of freedom of expression and put a stop to

modern censorship (American Library Association). *Is there a web address?*

In analyzing the history behind the banning of novels like Adventures of

Huckleberry Finn and Of Mice and Men, we can see a pattern that is very likely to repeat

itself with the modern example of the Harry Potter series. Subjects, themes and images

which were once considered taboo are now seen as everyday content in modern literature

and the media. Up until today, there is no definitive proof that Harry Potter contains

underlying messages that would corrupt the younger audiences that read the series.

However, if it were to be proven that these subliminal messages do exist in these books,

it is only to the eyes of the present society that bases its vision on current values of

morality. History has proven that this morality changes and evolves with time, and even

if Harry Potter is taken out of the shelves today, decades from now, it could be considered another classic, just like many other books banned throughout the course of time.

Works Cited

American Library Association. 2008. April 2008. <http://www.ala.org>.

"Ban Harry Potter or Face More School Shootings." Daily Mail 4 April 2006. 3 March

    2008 <http://www.dailymail.co.uk/pages/live/articles/news/worldnews/

    .html?in_article_id=408490&in_page_id=1811>.

"JK Rowling Outs Dumbledore as Gay" BBC News 20 Oct 2007. 2 April 2008 <http://

    news.bbc.co.uk/go/pr/fr/-/2/hi/entertainment/7053982.stm>.

Kennedy, Elizabeth. "Banning and Censorship of Children's Books." About.com 10

    April 2008 <http://childrensbooks.about.com/cs/censorship/a/censorship.

    htm>.

Mackay, Neil. "Witches' War with Church for Kids' Souls." The Sunday Herald 6 Aug

    2000. ProQuest. Miami-Dade College, Miami, FL. 2 April 2008

    <http://www.findarticles.com>.

McDougall, Liam. "Harry Potter the New Gay Icon?" The Sunday Herald 13 July 2003.

    ProQuest. Miami-Dade College, Miami, FL. 14 Mar 2008 <http://www.find

    articles.com>.

Mullaly, Claire. "Banned Books." First Amendment Center 4 Jan 2007. 14 April 2008

    <http://www.firstamendmentcenter.org/Speech/libraries/topic.aspx?topic=ban

    ned_books>.

Newth, Mette. "The Long History of Censorship." Beacon for Freedom of Expression

    17 April 2008 <http://www.beaconforfreedom.org/about_project/history.html>.

Chapter **5**

Final Steps
of the Research Process

Understanding and effectively formatting the research paper material requires practice. There will always be some style-specific issue that needs to be looked up, and there are several Web sites, along with your handbook, that can help in the page formatting. There are even a few Web-based programs that can format your works cited page for you. However, at the end of the day, if you do not know what you are entering into those programs or Web sites, it can still come out wrong.

Formatting Guidelines

In-Text Citations

The following set of notes is meant for you to be able to quickly review the rules of the Modern Language Association (MLA) for in-text citations. It is not meant to replace reading the handbook or being in class for lecture. Very specific minor details to this style will come more easily with regular practice and use in your work.

In-text citations are facts, quotes, or details that come from sources that are included in a body of original writing such as an essay or research paper. *Note:* For more reading, see pages 517–529 in the *Bedford Handbook.* The examples that follow are the most common types of citations used by students and correspond with numbers 1, 2, 3, 6, 7, and 23. Important note: The examples below are direct quotes, but even if you paraphrase an author's ideas, you still need to cite. You would simply leave out the quotation marks.

- *Author named in parenthesis:* When you are quoting or paraphrasing what an author says or a fact he or she has given, but you have not yet stated his or her name in the sentence, you include the author's last name in the parentheses. *Note:* "Author LN" refers to author's last name. Also, pg simply stands for page number, but you would not use this abbreviation in a citation; it would simply be the number itself.

    Remember: If you do not have the original page numbers of the work, MLA states it is not included.

    One author → "Blah blah blah" (Author LN pg).

    Two authors → "Blah blah blah" (Author LN and Author LN pg).

    Three authors → "Blah blah blah" (Author LN, Author LN, and Author LN pg).

    Four or more authors → "Blah blah blah" (Author LN et al. pg).

Indirect source, the original author or authors quote someone else → According to person who made statement, "Blah blah blah" (qtd. in Author LN pg). *Note:* This example is from an article with one author; if there are multiple authors for an article, use the examples above to guide you, but be sure to write the "qtd in" prior to listing them.

Unknown author → "Blah blah blah" ("Part of Title" pg).

- *Author named in a signal phrase:* If you have already used the author's name in the sentence, then the parentheses at the end only include the page number.

One author → According to Author LN, "Blah blah blah" (pg).

Two authors → According to Author LN and Author LN, "Blah blah blah" (pg).

Three authors → According to Author LN, Author LN, and Author LN, "Blah blah blah" (pg).

Four or more authors → According to Author LN et al. "Blah blah blah" (pg).

Some other very specific elements about in-text citations follow.

- There is no punctuation when you close the quote or paraphrase before the parenthesis symbol unless it is a ! or a ?.
- Capitalize the author's last name.
- There is no comma between author's last name and page number.
- If there are two authors, use the word "and" in between last names, not the symbol "&."
- If there are three authors, use commas after the first and second authors' last names.
- There should be no "p" or "pg" to indicate page number; it should just be the number.
- Put a period after you close the parentheses.
- If you have two authors with the same last name, include the first initial of each author's name to distinguish them.
- If you have two or more works in one citation, list them in alphabetical order, separated by a ; in the parenthesis.

Worksheet—In-Text Citations

Name _____   **Date** _____

Carefully review the formatting guidelines in this chapter, as well as your handbook or a reliable website such as OWL for formatting guidelines, and use them to complete the following exercises.

Create an in-text citation for each of the following types of sources. Double-check your work with the handbook, a classmate, and your instructor. Once you start doing in-text citations regularly, you will start to see the pattern repeating and you will always know what to look for, regardless of the type of source you need to cite.

Direct Quote, One Author, Author Named in Parenthesis

_____

_____

Direct Quote, Three Authors, Authors Named in Signal Phrase

_____

_____

Paraphrase, Two Authors, Authors Named in Signal Phrase

_____

_____

Direct Quote, Indirect Source, One Author, Author Named in Parenthesis

_____

_____

Paraphrase, Four or more Authors, Authors Named in Parenthesis

_____

_____

Paraphrase, Four or more Authors, Authors Named in Signal Phrase

_____

_____

Direct Quote, One Author (But Have Another Author with Same Last Name in List of Sources), Author Named in Parenthesis

_____

_____

Direct Quote, Three Authors and One Author (two different works), Authors Named in Parenthesis

_____

_____

Paraphrase, Two Authors, Authors Named in Parenthesis

_____

_____

Works Cited Entries

Again, the following set of notes is meant for you to be able to quickly review the rules of MLA for works cited entries. It is not meant to replace reading the handbook or being in class for lecture. Very specific minor details to this style will come more easily with regular practice and use in class.

Works cited are a list of sources from which quotes, paraphrases, facts, statistics, or details were excerpted and put in the body of the originally created work, such as an essay or research paper. *Note:* For more reading, refer to pages 529–568 in the *Bedford Handbook.* The following examples illustrate the most common types of sources used by students, which correspond with the numbers 1, 8, 25, 27, 35, and 40.

- *Book with one author*

    Author LN, FN. *Title of Book.* City of Publication: Publisher, Year. Medium.

- *Book with an author and an editor*

    Author LN, FN. Title of Book. Ed. Editor's Name. City of Publication: Publisher, year. Medium.

- *Article in a journal that has volumes and issues*

    Author LN, FN. "Title of Article." *Title of Journal* vol.iss (date): page-page. Medium.

- *Article in a weekly magazine*

    Author LN, FN and FN LN. "Title of Article." *Title of Magazine* day month year: page-page. Medium.

- *Article from an online Web site*

    Author LN, FN. "Title of Article." *Title of Web Site.* Sponsor, Day month year of update. Medium. Day month year of access.

- *A work from an online service to which your library subscribes*

    Author LN, FN. "Title of Article." *Title of Journal* volume.issue (date): page-page. *Title of Database.* Medium. Day Month Year of access.

Following are some specific elements to notice within a works cited page.

- If there is more than one author of a work, only the first author is put in the order of last name, first name. The second and subsequent authors get their names written in regular order. Example: Smith, James R. and Maria L. Gonzalez.
- There is a period at the end of the author(s). There is also a period at the end of titles within the quotation marks.
- Titles of books, magazines, journals, databases and Web sites are underlined or in italics with no period at the end.
- When you have volume and issue numbers, the date goes in parentheses.
- If there are no page numbers for an online source, indicate it by writing n. pag.
- If there is no updated date listed on a Web site, indicate it by writing n.d.

- No little letters are used for page numbers, volume numbers, or issue numbers; in other words, no little p, pg, v, vol, i, or iss.
- When you have the day, month, and year, you always put the day first. If you want to abbreviate the month, it should be the first three letters of the month and a period.
- If you only have the year as a date, then only put the year. If you have a season such as Summer or Fall and year, then you may abbreviate that as well. *Do not omit any part of the date given on a source.*
- For Web sites, you need the author of the article on the Web site as well as the editor or Web master of the site, the company sponsoring the site, and the date the site was last revised if it is available.
- If a works cited entry wraps around to the next line, the second line onward is indented five spaces.
- All entries in a works cited page should be arranged in alphabetical order according to the last name of the first author of each source. If a work does not have any authors, then the first letter of the title will dictate its place in the works cited list.

Worksheet—Works Cited

Name _____ **Date** _____

Carefully review the formatting guidelines in this chapter, as well as your handbook, and use them together to complete the following exercises.

Create a works cited entry for each of the following, and then create a works cited page. Double-check your work with the handbook, a classmate, and your instructor. Once you do a few works cited entries correctly, you will start to see the pattern repeating and you will always know what to look for, regardless of what type of source you need to cite.

1. A book with one author

   _____

   _____

2. A book chapter with two authors and two book editors (different from the chapter authors)

   _____

   _____

3. An article in a monthly journal with three authors

   _____

   _____

4. An article in a weekly magazine with one author

   _____

   _____

5. An article from an online database with five authors

   _____

   _____

6. A Web site article with its own author

_____

_____

7. An article from an online database with two authors and no page numbers listed

_____

_____

8. A website article with its own author, sponsoring institution, and no last updated date available

_____

_____

APA, American Psychological Association

The following review is meant for you to be able to quickly grasp the general rules of APA for in-text citations and works cited entries. It is not meant to replace reading your handbook or reviewing formatting websites for specific assistance. This is just a general overview of the style that will come more easily with regular practice and use in class.

Remember that in-text citations are facts, quotes, or details that come from sources that are included in a body of writing originally created such as an essay or research paper. For more reading, see pages 639–644 in the *Bedford Handbook.* The examples below correspond with numbers 2, 3, 4, 5 and 13.

Author not named: (When you are quoting or paraphrasing what an author says or a fact he/she has given, but you have not stated his/her name in the sentence yet with any kind of signal phrase, you include the author(s) LN in the parenthesis along with the year of the publication; also note that if it is a direct quote, you would also include the page number.)

Note: Author LN refers to Author's Last Name.

One author → "Yada yada yada" (Author LN, yr, p.#).

Two authors → "Yada yada yada" (Author LN & Author LN, yr, p.#).

Three to five authors → "Yada yada yada" (Author LN, Author LN, & Author LN, yr, p.#).

Six or more authors → "Yada yada yada" (Author LN et al., yr, p.#).

The original author(s) quotes someone else → According to person who made statement, "Yada yada yada" (as cited in Author LN, yr, p.#).

Author named: (If you have already used the author's name in the sentence with a signal phrase, then the year goes next to the author's name in parenthesis; if it is a direct quote, the parenthesis at the end only includes the page number.)

One author → According to Author LN (yr), "Yada yada yada" (p.#).

Two authors → According to Author LN and Author LN (yr), "Yada yada yada" (p.#).

Three to five authors → According to Author LN, Author LN, and Author LN (yr), "Yada yada yada" (p.#).

Six or more authors → According to Author LN et al. (yr), "Yada yada yada" (p.#).

You also want to notice very specific elements about in-text citations such as:

- There is no punctuation when you close the quote or before the parenthesis unless it is a ! or ? in the direct quote.
- You capitalize the author's last name(s).
- There is a comma between author's last name and the year.
- If there are two or more authors, use the word and in between last names in the signal phrase, but use the symbol & when their names are in the parenthesis.
- If there are three to five authors, use commas after each author's last name.
- If it is a direct quote without a signal phrase, there should be a page number after the year; if it is a summary or paraphrase, only the author and year is required.
- Put a period after you close the parenthesis.

APA References

Again, the following set of guidelines is meant for you to be able to quickly review the rules of APA references entries. As before, specific patterns will emerge that you will become accustomed to as you work with this style.

References are a list of sources from which quotes, paraphrases, facts, statistics, or details were consulted and used to support the body of the originally created work, such as an essay or research paper.

For more reading, refer to pages 645–669 in the Bedford Handbook. The examples below illustrate numbers 1, 7, 8, 34, and 39. Note: FI refers to 'First Initial'. APA usually lists only the last names of authors and then first initials (and middle initials if they have them).

- *Book with one author:*

  Author LN, FI. (year). *Title of book.* City of Publication, State: Publisher.

- *Article in a journal that has volumes and issues:*

  Author LN, FI. (year). Title of article. *Title of Journal, vol* (iss), page-page.

- *Article in a weekly magazine:*

  Author LN, FI., & LN, FI. (year, Month). Title of article. *Title of Magazine, vol* (iss), page-page.

- *A work from an online service to which your library subscribes:*

  Author LN, FI. (year). Title of article. *Title of Journal, vol* (iss), page-page. doi: or Retrieved from url

- *Article from an online website:*

  Author LN, FI. (year, Month). Title of article. Retrieved from url

Some specific elements to notice within references:

- If there is more than one author of a work, each author is listed by last name, and first initial. Ex. Smith, J. R. & Gonzalez, M. L.
- There is a period after (year).
- Titles of books, magazines, newspapers and journals are italicized with a period at the end.
- When you have volume and issue numbers, the issue goes in parenthesis after the volume.
- No little letters are used for volume numbers or issue numbers; in other words, no little v, vol, i, or iss; it is just the number.
- When you have the day, month, and year, include all parts of the date, with the year first. (For example: (2002, December).) If you only have the year as a date, then only put the year. If you have a season such as Summer or Fall and year, then you may include that as well. *Do not omit any part of the date given on a source.*
- For a database article, you list the doi if it is given; if not, you list the home web address of the journal.
- For any web address (url), there is no period listed at the end of the address.
- If a reference source wraps around to the next line, the 2nd line onward is indented five spaces.
- All entries in a references page should be arranged in alphabetical order according to the last name of the first author of each source.

Checklist

After you finish drafting your paper, and you have double-checked all of the content, in-text citations, and works cited information, it is time to write another draft. Still, that second draft may not be the final draft. It is important to review any draft (and ideally have someone else look at your draft as well) for the following items. Notice how this checklist will take you from the beginning to the end of the paper if you truly use it.

✓ MLA format of the overall document correct? Margins, spacing, running header, page numbers, heading (your name, professor name, class, date), centered title, paragraph indent. (Be sure in-text citations are correct if/when used.)

✓ Thesis statement effective and accurate? Address the topic + main idea + point A + point B + point C (if you are doing an explicit thesis), one sentence, third person.

✓ Clarity of thesis wording, easily understood concept, parallel structure?

✓ Quality of introduction? History/background, definitions, interesting quotes/statistics, general debates, transition to thesis.

✓ Grammar/syntax level in introduction? Commas, subject/verb agreement, verb tenses, fragments, run-ons, spelling, and so on.

✓ Is the body section organized according to the thesis statement or a logical emphatic order? (In other words, does reason A have its own section? Does reason B's section automatically follow A, and so forth? If not an explicit thesis, does each section develop its own point, increasing in importance?)

✓ Does the development of the body sections show order of emphasis? (In other words, is reason C the "most" developed? Is reason B more developed than A but less than C? Is reason A the "least" developed?)

✓ Is each body section sufficiently supported with clear in-text citations using authors reflected in the works cited page?

✓ Does the end of each body section refer back to the overall main idea in the thesis statement?

✓ Grammar/syntax level of body section? Commas, subject/verb agreement, verb tenses, fragments, run-ons, spelling, and so forth.

✓ MLA format correct for in-text citations in body?

✓ If it's an argumentative paper, is the opposing argument correct? One opposing idea, explained fully, support if you have it.

✓ Rebuttal correct? Specifically addresses the opposing idea, has multiple support, fully explained, interesting.

✓ Restatement of thesis accurate and effective? Addresses the topic + main idea + point A + point B + point C (again, if meant to be an explicit thesis), one sentence, third person (not repeated exactly as thesis, starts conclusion).

✓ Quality of conclusion? Thoughtful closing, explains why this topic is important in society or prediction, charge to action, quotes, statistics, question and answer. Be sure the last line is in your own words.

✓ Grammar/syntax level of conclusion? Commas, subject/verb agreement, verb tenses, fragments, run-ons, spelling, and so on.

If you are satisfied with the work you have done, and you have received feedback from your peers, instructor, *and* yourself, then it is time to write that final draft. This should be it!

Proofreading Tips

Once you have the final draft, you then settle yourself down for proofreading. A few tips follow.

- Once your draft is done, print it out. (It will be much more effective than trying to read the computer screen after being on the computer for a long period of time.) Then walk away from it for at least thirty minutes.

- Return to the paper and review the overall structure. Make sure you have followed the right organization.

- Check each section of the paper with a colored pen. Be sure you have followed all of the directions. Be sure you have reviewed every checklist and received feedback and have revised.

- Check for unity, development, and coherence in each paragraph. Be especially sure to have enough support for each point. If the support is short, think about what you can explain further. Revisit your index cards to see if there is something else you can include that would lend stronger support.

- Check the MLA style of the paper. Be sure you have noted all the fine details. See the *Little, Brown Handbook,* the *Bedford Handbook,* or your notes if you are unsure.

- Start final proofreading. Correct grammar and syntax. See your previous writings for skills you have had problems with in the past. Check the *Little, Brown Handbook,* the *Bedford Handbook,* and/or sit with a peer in order to not repeat the same errors.

- Go back to your typed draft and edit your paper, making all necessary corrections. Print out and save a complete and beautifully written/constructed paper!

- Submit your paper and get some rest!

Glossary

abstract—A summary of the research paper. An abstract often appears before the complete research article in professional journals. It provides an overview of the primary findings of the researcher. An abstract does not suffice as a resource by itself.

access date—The date on which you located the information from a Web site or electronic service. It is not the date on which the article was published.

anthology—A collection of articles, essays, poems, or stories assembled by an editor and published as one book. Each selection in an anthology has its own title and author.

APA—American Psychological Association, which requires its own specific method of documenting a research paper. It is used in such disciplines as education, history, and social science.

bibliography card—An index card on which you record all the publication information that will eventually become part of your paper's works cited page.

blog—This is now the accepted word for "web log," an essay or analysis that appears as a regular column on the internet.

citation—The place in the paper that identifies the source of the information you just used. It appears in parentheses immediately after you use the information or idea. Different types of sources require different citation formats; check your handbook for proper format.

cite—To tell the reader where you found the information when you use that information in your paper.

city of publication—The city in which the book was published. It appears on the title page.

combination note card—a note card that is part paraphrase (in the student's own words) and part direct quotation (word for word from the original source).

consecutive citation—A citation of one source followed immediately by another citation from the same source. If you cite material from Jones and in the next paragraph you cite material from Jones again with no other source used between the two, you have consecutive citations. In this case, you do not need to repeat the name Jones in parentheses; you merely include the page number because the reader will know the source itself has not changed.

database—A catalog of sources assembled by a service to ease the retrieval of articles by subject, author, or title. Examples include Wilson Web, Academic Search Premier, and OmniFile.

direct quotation—Using a word-for-word sentence, phrase, or passage from a source in your paper and enclosing it in quotation marks without any additions or changes.

documentation—The identification of the sources used in a paper, covering both the internal references within the paper itself and the list of works cited that appears at the paper's end.

dropped quotation—A quotation without proper signal phrase; it seems miraculously "dropped" into the paper. Avoid this.

editor—The person who compiles an anthology and writes introductory material and commentary before and after the individual works.

electronic journal—A journal found only on the Web.

ellipsis—Three dots that indicate the omission of information in a quotation.

et al.—"And others." This is used after the first author in a works cited page when the source has four or more authors instead of typing the names of all of the authors.

indirect quotation—Rephrasing a quotation into a paraphrase; often prefaced by the word "that." For example, *He said, "I will not raise taxes"* becomes *He said that he would not raise taxes.*

internal citation—See **in-text citation.**

in-text citation—Identifying the author and page number of material immediately after its use within the body of the research paper. Also called *parenthetical citation* or *internal citation.*

issue—The individual publication identified by either date, season, or number. Popular magazines publish weekly or monthly issues; scholarly and professional journals often publish seasonal or numbered issues.

magazine—A popular publication issued at regular intervals.

MLA—Modern Language Association, which requires a particular method of documentation used in the humanities (English and foreign language, for example).

newspaper—A daily or weekly publication, usually regional, although it can be discipline specific (*The Chronicle of Higher Education,* for example). Common newspaper titles include *Times, Herald, Star, Chronicle, Journal, News, Post, Gazette.*

note card—An index card on which you record information as direct quotation, paraphrase, or summary.

online journal—See **electronic journal.**

pagination—The way the pages of a publication or paper are numbered.

paraphrase—Converting borrowed information into your own words while retaining the integrity of the original statement. *Note:* You are required to cite your source when you paraphrase to avoid plagiarism.

parenthetical citation—See **in-text citation.**

periodical—A publication issued at regular intervals, for example, a newspaper, magazine, or journal.

publication date—The date the article originally appeared in a periodical.

publisher—The company that produced a book. It is found on the title page.

quotation within a quotation—Occurs when you lift material in which the author is quoting someone else in the article. The rule for this is to use double quotation marks (" ") around the entire passage and single quotation marks (' ') around the original quotation. There are specific MLA guidelines to cite this correctly in text. See your handbook or notes for specifics.

reference book—A dictionary, encyclopedia, thesaurus, or similar source.

resource—Source, place, and publication from which a researcher acquires information.

RSS—Ready Simple Solution, a type of "feed" that eases publication and updates of web information such as blogs and headlines.

signal phrase—A verb phrase that tells the reader to expect a quotation or paraphrase; an attribution to a source woven into a sentence.

source—The place of origin of information used in a research paper: article, book, Web site, interview. Also called a **resource.**

thesis statement—The sentence in the paper's introduction that identifies the subject of the research paper and provides a plan for its support.

title page—The page in a book that identifies the author, city of publication, publisher, and copyright year.

URL—A Web address. Uniform Resource Locator.

volume—A number that indicates the time a publication has been issued. For example, a journal numbered Volume 54 shows that it is in its fifty-fourth year of publication. The issue number usually follows the volume number. Volume 54, Number 5 means that this is the fifth issue published this year, which is the fifty-fourth year of publication.

works cited page—The page on which all the sources used in the paper are properly identified. This is the final page of the research paper and is numbered sequentially along with all the other pages in the paper. If you write a six-page paper, your works cited page becomes page 7.

Appendix

Name _____ **Date** _____

Posttest

1. What does MLA stand for?

   _____

   _____

   _____

2. How do you list the authors in a works cited page when you have two authors?

   _____

   _____

   _____

3. What is an academic database?

   _____

   _____

   _____

4. Write the title of an article you have retrieved from a database.

   _____

   _____

   _____

5. Write the journal/magazine title of one of your researched articles.

   _____

   _____

   _____

6. What does *parenthetical* or *internal citation* mean?

_____

_____

_____

7. What is the definition of *plagiarism?*

_____

_____

_____

8. What is a *signal phrase?*

_____

_____

_____

9. Directly quote two or three lines from one of your researched articles.

_____

_____

_____

10. Using a signal phrase, paraphrase the quotation from question 9.

_____

_____

_____

11. How are the entries arranged on a works cited page?

_____

_____

_____

12. What is the difference between a journal and a magazine?

_____

_____

_____

13. What is a periodical?

_____

_____

_____

14. What does "et al." mean?

_____

_____

_____

15. What type of documentation style will your research paper follow?

_____

_____

_____

16. What is the proper way to indent a works cited entry?

_____

_____

_____

17. Give an example of a parenthetical citation.

_____

_____

_____

18. What is the MLA capitalization rule for article titles?

_____

_____

_____

19. What is never an accepted source in scholarly research?

_____

_____

_____

20. Why is Wikipedia not usually considered the most valid and reliable source of information on which to base research papers?

_____

_____

_____

DISCARD